STRONGER

BUILDING A POWERFUL INTERIOR WORLD

By Jarrod Cooper

deep blue

Jarrod Cooper
Deep Blue Publishing
c/o Revive Church
Ashcombe Road
Kingston upon Hull
HU7 3DD
UK.

Where you see * you can find the basis for the illustration at www.sermonillustrations.com

** Source/author unknown.

ISBN: 9781791864934

Cover Design by VictoriaCooper
Image from Pixabay

DEDICATION

I dedicate this newly expanded edition of Stronger to the people who help me daily to be strong. My wife Victoria, whose endless kindness lifts me day after day. My son Zachary, who has shown me what a father's love feels like, giving me fresh hope in my Heavenly Father's love for me. My extended family who care, advise, inspire and uplift me. To my church family at Revive Church, who allow me to be pioneering, prophetic, slightly dysfunctional and refreshingly normal, all at the same time. Thank you for being a perfect church home for a mad-cap leader like me! And finally, to Jesus, God the Father and the Holy Spirit – Where would I be without the limitless ocean of Your grace! I have all eternity to sail it, and I know I will never find it's end! What a wonder?!

CONTENTS

Introduction

1   Weakness is Boring!   1

2   The Power of Perseverance   6

3   Don't Run From Resistance   11

4   The Flexible Flourish   19

5   Building a Firm Foundation   26

6   The Power of your Thoughts   33

7   Embarrass sin before it embarrasses you!   42

8   Living in your grace zone   50

9   Two are better   55

10 Skill magnifies strength   63

11 The Power of habit   70

12 Clothed with strength   81

    40 Day Devotional   93

    About the Authors   199

Introduction

I recently discovered I needed to get stronger.

Ever been there? Where your own weakness is starting to really frustrate you? You suddenly realise, things aren't going to get easier so you might as well stop praying for easy times – We just need to get stronger!

I'd been in ministry 25 years, had all sorts of adventures and fun, seen God do amazing miracles, save lives and move powerfully by His presence. But then I went through one of the most difficult, dark seasons of my life.

It was in this time I discovered that gifting and charisma was one thing, but perseverance and toughness to see a vision fulfilled was another. I learned that while vision and dreams are really important – without greater strength I simply wasn't going to complete all God had for me.

Maybe like me, you have a vision, but you can also be quite insecure. Perhaps you have gifts from God, and yet you're thin-skinned and easily offended, and this rocks you to your core. Are you too easily distracted, discouraged, ill-disciplined or just ill?

Maybe you're realising that finishing this race isn't going to be nearly as easy, fun or dreamy, as starting it! Well, that's exactly what this little book is about.

My friend, pastor and musician Dave Hind, wrote a beautiful song:

So many lost, casualties, on the journey
Some who once ran strong, now gone, where did they go wrong?
How we need your grace, how we need your strength
Please carry me
Tragedies, on the road, on the journey
Some who turn and choose another path, and lose their way
And oh without your grace, we can't make it on our own
Please carry me

To finish strong
To not lose the way, is my greatest desire
To speak your name, with my final breath
Will be my finest hour
Please don't let me run if I've not learnt to walk
Don't let me shout, if I've not learned to talk
I never want to leave the Way

It's not how you start, how fast you run, but finish the race
It's not if you win, if you try, but pass the test
Your grace it helps us stand
We finish in your arms
Please carry me

Don't give me riches, Don't give me poverty
Give me my daily bread
Don't give me fame, if it means I will lose you I long,
I crave, my passion, to finish strong.

If you've lost your way, lost your faith, lost your hope
Don't know where you are, what went wrong
Can't find the way home
His grace is enough, His love still stands.
He'll carry you.

Perhaps, like me and my friend David, you are beginning to realise that starting the race was the easy bit. Building genuine strength and resilience for the journey is now necessary to complete this race, without getting shipwrecked along the way.

This little book is all about where we find strength. You see, God provides us with "strength builders" along our path – some we need to pick up and use, others will simply happen to us along the way, by a kind of divine providence. But knowing these seasons of muscle building are from heaven ('cos they usually look like they're from hell at first!) is vital to recognising God's plan for your resilience.

If you have a desire to develop strength for your life – to protect your marriage or enjoy singleness, to fulfill your vision or grow your career, to enjoy a long life and keep your integrity, then read on. I've written this just for you!

Chapter One: Weakness Is Boring!

"Let the weak say, 'I am strong!'" Joel 3:10

I'm bored of weakness.

I sometimes think that we love the revelation that WE ARE WEAK, but forget that HE IS STRONG in us!

Perhaps we want to avoid the responsibility of becoming strong, capable, influential, of enduring the inevitable pressures of success. It's a false, lazy kind of humility.

Truly, the shine has worn off weakness for me.

Joel 3:10 says, *"Let the weak say, 'I am strong!'"*

If we only embraced the first half of the statement, we will forever be weak, vacillating, fearful, shamed versions of the mighty men and women of God He intends us to be. The men and women Jesus shed His blood to bring into salvation and glory! He didn't die for you to stay weak – He died to turn the weak one into a strong one!

So, I think it is time for the weak to say, I AM STRONG.

I think it's time for us to step into part two of that saying, and be mighty, clothed in His strength, in His righteousness, in His grace!

It is time for the weak knees to be strengthened, for the fearful hearts to hear that you can "Be strong, your God will come to save you!" (Isaiah 35:4).

In the first chapter of Joshua, four times it says, in various ways,

"Be BOLD, be STRONG, be COURAGEOUS" and even "BE VERY COURAGEOUS!"

There is no way you can enter the fullness of your destiny without becoming strong and courageous!

In Phil Pringle's fabulous book "The 10 Qualities of a Great Leader" he says the simple yet profound statement:

"The STRONG can do what the weak cannot."

He is pointing out the blindingly obvious, yet constantly forgotten truth, that the strong will resist what the weak don't.

The strong keep going, when the weak give up.

The strong resist temptation, the weak give in.

The strong remain in peace, while the weak stumble, are thrown off, and fall.

The strong turn up when the weak give up.

The strong carry heavy weights, while the weak drop responsibilities.

The strong control their emotions, while the weak are overcome by stress.

The strong draw meekness and humility out of their grace filled souls, while the weak are overcome by ego, approval addiction and ambition.

The strong do not dwell on issues they cannot change, while the weak are overcome by regret, shame and the disapproval of others.

The strong attend when the weak fall away.

The strong break through, clear the way, endure hard times…while the weak fail, shipwrecked by little irritations and inconveniences.

The strong rise up, attack, take ground, advance, improve, update, embrace change. While the weak hide, searching for the path of least resistance, cost and pain.

The strong embrace all God has for them, while the weak fall away in fear and are forgotten.

I do not want to be weak any more! How about you?

You Are My Son
At a very low point in my life, when I was feeling pretty weak and feeble, God came to me in a vision. He stood before me as a mighty warrior, literally as tall as a skyscraper. He raised His arms to heaven, raised His head and shouted out loudly "You are My son! You are My son!"

Various thoughts rushed around my mind, verses like "The Lord is a Warrior" (Exodus 15:3) and the beautiful approving words the Father spoke over Jesus as His ministry began:

"You are my Son, whom I love; with you I am well pleased" Luke 3:22.

But the most powerful realisation I had in that moment was that I was God's son, and He was mighty, not weak! I indeed felt weak, shamed, stupid, defeated - but He was crying shamelessly out to the heavens "You are My son!" – In other words, "I am your Father, you have My genes, My might is running in your spiritual veins; My power is available to you! This is the family you come from. Stop focusing on your weakness, inability, sinfulness – start to focus on what you have inherited – a glorious strength, grace, power and potency from heaven!"

When I checked out the word "weak" in a thesaurus it says things like breakable, delicate, sickly, unwell, invalid, ineffective, unsound, inadequate, unsatisfactory, foolish, stupid, vacillating, wavering, unstable, irresolute, fluctuating, inconsiderable, flimsy, poor, trivial, lacking.

I do NOT want to be that guy!

In turn, I looked up the word STRONG:

Mighty, sturdy, brawny, sinewy, hardy, muscular, stout, potent, capable, efficient, valiant, brave, bold, persuasive, impressive, steady, firm, secure, unwavering, resolute, resilient.

Now that's who I want to be! That's what I want on my gravestone, OK!

Think of all our biblical and historical heroes; aren't they summed up by the second list, not the first?

In fact, to get to the very heart of the issue, didn't many start out as the first list, and somehow became the second?

Well, that is what we are going to learn in the following chapters. If any of us are starting out on the first list, then we are going to discover together how to become the second list...the list of the MIGHTY. With God's grace, with God's mercy, with God's principles you too can become strong and effective.

For Group Discussion:

1. Do you agree that people use weakness as an excuse for not living in God's best?

2. How different could your life be, if you lived it strong instead of weak? What would change?

3. Do you think there is a difference between your opinion of yourself, and God's opinion? If so, describe the difference.

4. Has anyone in the group ever worked through a certain weakness, to become strong? Tell your story.

Chapter Two: The Power Of Perseverance

"By perseverance the snail reached the Ark." Spurgeon

One of the great attributes of strength is perseverance. Someone once said, "Postage stamps are getting more expensive, but at least they have one attribute that most of us could emulate: they stick to one thing until they get there."

There is something about perseverance that makes us unquenchable, unstoppable, and therefore helps us to live significant lives.

The Bible has much to say about perseverance, about refusing to quit, in order to fulfil destiny:

*"Consider it pure joy, my brothers, whenever you face trials of
many kinds, because you know that the testing of your
faith develops perseverance. Perseverance must finish its work so
that you may be mature and complete, not lacking anything."*
James 1:2-4

*"Blessed is the man that endures temptation: for when he is tried,
he shall receive the crown of life, which the Lord has promised to
them that love him."* James 1:12

"So do not throw away your confidence; it will be richly

rewarded. You need to persevere so that when you have done the will of God, you will receive what he has promised." Hebrews 10:35-36.

"And let us not be weary in well doing: for in due season we shall reap, if we faint not." Galatians 6:9

Calvin Coolidge once wrote *"Nothing in this world can take the place of persistence. Talent will not; nothing is more common than unsuccessful men with talent. Genius will not; unrewarded genius is almost a proverb. Education will not; the world is full of educated derelicts. Persistence and determination alone are omnipotent. The slogan "press on" has solved and always will solve the problems of the human race."*

Persistence is part of the world of all the "Greats" of history. To do anything worthwhile, you must be someone who not only starts well, (Oh, most do this!) but continue, through trial, setback, pressure, conflict and utter failure, yet keep going.

Can you guess whose life this is a summary of?

Failed in business, aged 22
Ran for Legislature—defeated, aged 23
Again failed in business, aged 24
Elected to Legislature, aged 25
Sweetheart died, aged 26
Had a nervous breakdown, aged 27
Defeated for Speaker, aged 29
Defeated for Elector, aged 31
Defeated for Congress, aged 34
Elected to Congress, aged 37
Defeated for Congress, aged 39
Defeated for Senate, aged 46
Defeated for Vice President, aged 47
Defeated for Senate, aged 49
Elected President of the United States, aged 51 *

Those are the headlines of Abraham Lincoln's life! Can you imagine what history would have been like if he'd have given up at his first defeat, when he lost his sweetheart, or when he had a nervous breakdown? We must learn to endure if we are going to live a great life.

John Wesley's diary has a remarkable month in it that I find so inspiring:

Sunday, A.M., May 5
Preached in St. Anne's. Was asked not to come back anymore.

Sunday, P.M., May 5
Preached in St. John's. Deacons said "Get out and stay out."

Sunday, A.M., May 12
Preached in St. Jude's. Can't go back there, either.

Sunday, A.M., May 19
Preached in St. Somebody Else's. Deacons called special meeting and said I couldn't return.

Sunday, P.M., May 19
Preached on street. Kicked off street.

Sunday, A.M., May 26
Preached in meadow. Chased out of meadow as bull was turned loose during service.

Sunday, A.M., June 2
Preached out at the edge of town. Kicked off the highway

Sunday, P.M., June 2
Afternoon, preached in a pasture. Ten thousand people came out to hear me. *

Wow!

If Abraham Lincoln had given up after failing to be elected time and again, if Wesley had run from persecution or rejection, they would not have changed the world the way they did!

They changed the world because of their perseverance and strength.

Don't **Quit**

Joyce Meyer writes the following in her wonderful book, "A Leader in the Making":

"There were times when I had to face loneliness and hard work, times when I wanted to give up and quit. God kept putting people in my path I didn't want to deal with, but he placed them there because I needed them. They were the sandpaper I needed to rub off my rough edges.

"I struggled with the process of change for a long time, but I finally realised that God was not going to do things my way. He did not want an argument from me; He only wanted to hear, 'Yes Lord, Your will be done.'"

That is how it is in life. You are going to need to be strong enough to fulfil everything He made you to accomplish. Along the journey there will be setbacks, conflict, suffering and disappointment. But God will use every setback to perfect you, to make you like Christ, and to bring you to a place where you can express His glory in a magnificent destiny.

We cannot quit! We must endure in order to receive all that He has promised us.

So how can we become strong? How can we develop perseverance? How can we go from feeling weak to being resilient? Keep on reading…

For Group Discussion:

1. Why is perseverance necessary?

2. Calvin Coolidge once wrote, "Nothing in this world can take the place of persistence. Talent will not; nothing is more common than unsuccessful men with talent. Genius will not; unrewarded genius is almost a proverb. Education will not; the world is full of educated derelicts. Persistence and determination alone are omnipotent. The slogan "press on" has solved and always will solve the problems of the human race." Discuss.

3. Discuss the character traits that people like Abraham Lincoln and John Wesley must have had, to persevere through such difficulty and setbacks. How can you develop such traits in your own lives?

Chapter Three:
Don't Run From Resistance!

"Triumph is just "umph" added to try." Marvin Phillips

Strength comes from somewhere.

It doesn't just appear, it doesn't just drop out of the sky. It is carefully and purposefully developed in you.

The first place strength comes from is resistance.

Resistance Is Necessary
Quite simply resistance is that moment when you push back against something that is pushing against you.

Ask a weight lifter and he will tell you, it's all about RESISTANCE. Exerting force against something that is weighty causes you to build muscle and grow your strength and stamina. It is true of physical muscles, but it is also true of your spirit man, your soul, your mind and emotions.

And so God will let you experience resistance.

In most lives there are periods of fairly intense resistance that make us strong. At first it may seem that something is about to destroy you, but afterwards you realise, it kind of "made you!"

The young shepherd boy David defeated a lion, a bear, a giant, but then went on to face the giant of the jealous attacks of King Saul - all stages building resolve and God-dependence that would make him resilient for the future.

Joseph grew strong in the jail. Abraham grew strong in the desert. Moses grew strong by a failed attempt at destiny, then a long period of development as a shepherd.

If you read through the book of Judges you will soon realise that none of our heroes would have been great without an enemy, whose resistance made them great. Can you imagine Samson or Gideon without their enemies? We often fail to realise that the things that are resisting us, are the very things that are making us strong.

In Jesus's early life on earth, Luke 2:40 tells us that He "grew and became strong; He was filled with wisdom and the grace of God was on Him."

Note that even Jesus had to "become strong." It wasn't an automatic thing. He, no doubt, grew by life lessons, by the spiritual lessons of knowing His Father, and He grew in strength by being submissive to His parents. Who knows that growing in submission to parents is a kind of resistance that will grow the strength of your character? Namely, through growing humility by learning how to take an order!

Jesus faced the devil in Luke chapter four and came out of the desert in the power of the Holy Spirit. It was a final act of resistance that propelled Him into a stronger future.

The Divine Catapult

Sometimes God's workings are like a catapult. We think we are being held back, that someone or something is resisting us. We may feel that we are being overlooked, forgotten, dishonoured, criticised or corrected.

But actually when life starts to move backwards because of resistance, it is usually God doing a work in our life, rather like a catapult. He is pulling us back in order to propel us forward with new strength and energy.

The apostle Paul spoke often of sufferings and persecutions that made him strong and developed his character and prepared him for glory. He put it this way:

"We glory in our sufferings, because we know that suffering produces perseverance; perseverance, character; and character, hope." Romans 5:3-5

Remember this; suffering, in other words, resistance, produces strength. Now we don't usually think about that in the middle of the struggle, we just want to get out of the painful situation. But often God is using something to purify and strengthen us.

Conflict, rejection, accusation, persecution, misunderstanding, waiting, being overlooked, attacked, ridiculed - All these make us more Christ-like if we embrace them as a work of heaven to bring the humility of Christ out in us!

He'll even use things He hasn't personally sent to strengthen us, as He "works all things together for our good" (Romans 8:28). Even sickness, loss, pain and trauma – Your heavenly Father loves you to bits and doesn't send these things into your life, any more than you would wish them on your own children. But God won't waste a thing; He will use it all to build us stronger for the future.

The Path Of Right Resistance

So in life, don't aim for the path of least resistance. Oh I know we all want to – but don't. Realise that some resistance will do you good at times.

Don't be too easy on yourself in prayer, (get up early!) in your relationships, (go practice saying "Sorry!") Don't be lazy with your Bible, (set some fun reading and studying goals) your finance, (strengthen and check your heart with some generous, painful giving!) or your witnessing. (Pray for a divine conversation today!)

Choose to keep your heart stretched, your faith alive, your spiritual walk robust. Choose some resistance, like a period of fasting or extra prayer, even when life is easy, so that when life gets tough, you have some resilience built in.

A Zulu Tradition

In Zulu tradition they sometimes let the young men sleep on the edge of the village camp, near to the wild animals. When asked why, one chief simply said, "To keep them brave."

Do some things that keep you addressing your fears, your reticence, any natural inclination to take it too easy all the time.

I know that I easily veer towards taking it easy. My flesh is like gravity - pulling me down towards the path of least resistance, least work, least pressure sometimes. I want easy friends, easy prayers, easy study, easy giving and easy attendance. Anyone else?!

I want comfortable commitments and low-grade sacrifices.

But living like that will keep me weak, and most importantly, when a real crisis hits, I'll crumble!

Recognise The Testing When It Comes

James 1:12 says, *"Blessed is the one who perseveres under trial (or test) because, having stood the test, that person will receive the crown of life that the Lord has promised to those who love him."*

When you're going through a bad day – with someone at work in conflict with you, a financial worry, or you're feeling overlooked in some way – how often do we stop and ask, "Is this God testing my heart?"

When that leader accidentally leaves you off the rota, we take it personally and get in a huff. Perhaps God was just testing your motives? After all, Jesus taught us to take the least seat at the banquet – i.e. Don't insist on the best seats and the best opportunities. An attitude of entitlement is a form of pride.

When you don't get paid what you think you deserve, or fail to receive the honour or recognition you hoped for, remember God may have allowed it to happen to test why you are doing that thing in the first place.

I think sometimes we charge headlong into thoughts of getting our own back, getting what we think we deserve, or grasping for our rightful recognition – when actually God may be building some strong humility in us, for future use.

Think about some of the things you're going through right now, or have been through lately. Are they tests? Is God allowing little pockets of resistance in order to build your strength? The big question is, are you passing the tests? Or are you failing miserably, giving in to weak, under-developed attitudes?

God will make you wait, be misunderstood, be falsely accused, humbled, maligned, wait for financial provision, be overlooked for promotion – just to build strength in you. Trust me though, the reward is worth it when you do it God's way!

You see God is far more interested in making you strong and

Christ-like than He is in giving you gifts, like He's some kind of Father Christmas! It is nothing for Him to give you money, recognition, opportunity, influence; and He will do those things. But He is far more interested in making you Christ-like.

Romans 8:18 says, *"I consider that our present sufferings are not worth comparing with the glory that will be revealed in us."* Suffering always leads to glory, as the deep heart work of suffering prepares us for greater days. You must remember in Romans 8:29 Paul says, *"For those God foreknew he also predestined to be conformed to the image of his Son."* He is committed to making you just like Jesus – glorious, powerful, loving, and magnificent - through suffering.

Every piece of resistance will bring to light where you are not yet like Jesus, so that you can reject it, ask for divine grace and help, and let God work in you the nature of Christ.

So when resistance comes, don't fight it. Recognise it, use it, and pass the test.

79 Venues In 13 Years!
Rick Warren's Church, Saddleback, endured moving through 79 venues in their first 13 years of existence as a church – still growing to 10,000 members in that time! What kind of strength do you think was built through the resistance of swapping venues, setting up, taking down, and trying to keep track of where they were going to meet on any given Sunday, all in the days before the internet?

Some of our churches are weak simply because everything is so easy – and we nonchalantly go through our existence without really strengthening our muscles.

There is a choir in a church I know in Africa that meets through the night on Thursday nights to practice, as the church calendar is so busy! I wonder how many people want to be in THAT worship team?!

As a church leader I have come to realise that I cannot keep my people from everything that is hard and inconvenient, because it is the difficult things that make us strong as a family.

There are venue changes, staff changes, time changes, name changes, generation changes, new ideas, new places to reach and all of the resistance involved in that journey actually makes us all strong.

A church family pandered to by its leaders, will be weak. Let's build strong people, and strong churches, by refusing to always take the path of least resistance.

Remember, resistance will make us strong.

For Group Discussion:

1. Why is resistance important to our lives? What sorts of things could be classed as godly resistance?

2. Romans 5:3-5 says, "We glory in our sufferings, because we know that suffering produces perseverance; perseverance, character; and character, hope." How can we glory in our sufferings?

3. How can we learn to recognise that a testing time is from God?

4. God will let you experience resistance, just like David, Joseph and even Jesus. Can you describe a time in your life when resistance, or hard times, made you strong?

Chapter Four: The Flexible, Flourish!

"Be gifted with wise flexibility" Angelica Hopes

Brittle things are weak. They snap.

When we become brittle, we are weak.

Weak people are too easily offended. They struggle to embrace life's changes.

Life is full of change, and if you are not flexible, life will break you. When a single person becomes a married person, without flexibility they'll struggle. Why is it that they say the first year of married life is hell? It is because we are selfish and inflexible!

When we move from being a couple to having children, if you are not flexible it will exhaust you! I used to think Victoria and I were selfless, but then we had our son Zach, and I learned what selflessness was all about, usually at about three in the morning!

And there are many, many more stages in life where a flexible, strong heart is necessary. When your little children become teenagers, the day they ask for the car keys, the day they leave home, the day they start families of their own.

What about those times in life when your own job changes, when you move and your city changes, sometimes your entire country changes? Our churches change and life heads off in different directions, in ways not anticipated at all. All these can be times of crisis if we don't have flexibility built into our hearts.

Some Christians get offended when the meeting time is changed, the venue changed, the music changed, the pastor changed, the steward didn't smile.

Brittle people are weak, but flexibility makes you strong. You can bend with the winds of change and the winds of storms.

One pastor took on a historic church and within a few weeks, decided that the church organ would be better in a different part of the church hall. The rookie leader moved the organ and on the following Sunday was shocked to watch world war 3 break out in his congregation!

"But the organ is always that side" one cried. "My grandmother used to play that organ" another whined. "Now it's too loud on the other side of the sanctuary" said another. "I can't reach it to put the flowers on it!" sobbed another. Tears and tantrums followed until the brow beaten pastor moved the organ back.

Mischievously he decided to move the organ just one inch a week, until a month later it was exactly where he had placed it. Only this time, as the change had been gradual, no one noticed, nor seemed to mind.

"Oh I always thought it would look nice there," said one. "Glad you took my advice" said another.

"Oh don't the flowers look nice against that backdrop now."

"I love the resonance of the organ these days."

Weaklings! Had they been flexible, no war would have broken out in the first place!

Of course, it matters little where an organ is placed in a church sanctuary as far as I'm concerned, but the story speaks of a deeper inflexibility common in church life.

Inflexibility about simple things like hall layouts, also means that when a growing church has to move to multiple services, people break away from church in offence. When a church service is adjusted because of new believers, or a new group of youth joining the church, old brittle bucket-mouthed believers snap! They whine, complain and throw a wobbly! When something needs to be stopped to accommodate a new need, brittle people crack like twiglets.

And when we are inflexible we often break if life doesn't go our way. We snap and leave our close walk with God when we go through a hard time, a difficult diagnosis, a financial crisis, or we don't get the job we thought we were going to get. If God makes us wait longer than we want to, or fails to answer our prayers in the way we told Him to, we give up on Him and go try to make it on our own.

But flexibility is a better way.

Flourishing Like A Palm Tree
"The righteous will flourish like a palm tree" Psalm 92:12.

Flexibility makes you like a Palm. Do you know palms can lean right over until their tops are touching the ground – and yet spring right back when the high winds have passed?

In fact, whenever a palm leans right over, rather than get weaker, it's roots dig even deeper into the ground, and it gets stronger! Its flexibility makes it tougher, not weaker.

That's a picture of you and me. The only way to truly follow Jesus is to remain flexible.

In Mark 7:6-9 Jesus teaches, *"Isaiah was right when he prophesied about you hypocrites; as it is written: 'These people honour me with their lips, but their hearts are far from me. They worship me in vain; their teachings are but rules taught by men.' You have let go of the commands of God and are holding on to the traditions of men." And he said to them: "You have a fine way of setting aside the commands of God in order to observe your own traditions"*

Here Jesus teaches that we can easily set aside God's true commands, in preference for our own traditions. These are usually easy, cosy, imitations of religion. This makes us brittle and inflexible, as we set aside true relationship with God, and spend our lives defending our preferred traditions. It's dangerous, because it feels a little like true godliness, but it is far from God's heart.

Jesus said these people are hypocrites, literally actors, acting out a part in a play. He said, "they worship me in vain." Oh, they sing and pray about Jesus alright but they are inflexible, brittle, proud actors. Wow!

I heard of a church of 500 that moved from Asia to Europe en masse, at the word of the Lord coming to them in a prophecy. Could we ever be that obedient? That flexible? Or would we carry on play acting at church, drowning out the whispers of heaven by our churchy music and religious routines?

For a year a couple drove from Bristol to Hull every week for one of our evening Bible School classes. That's over 4 hours drive, each way! Yet there are some that won't drive 20 minutes or take a bus! That couple were flexible – most couldn't imagine bending their lives to accommodate such a thing.

There are churches today that start setting up at 6am on Sunday morning and run through until midnight. Could we be open to those levels of flexible, sacrificial service? Or are we caught in the cultural trap of considering whatever we do as "normal" and what others do as fanatical? It is always dangerous to consider ourselves the standard of "normal." It leaves you inflexible and weak.

Change Is Unchanging

Now I have sympathy with those who are inflexible, because change can be horrid. It makes us feel uncomfortable, inadequate and sweaty, or is that just me?!

When something changes, sometimes we go through the stages of grief – we have literally lost something and are bereaved in a way, even if it is quite minor.

But it is impossible to be strong, without embracing change, so the sooner we teach our hearts to trust God in change, the sooner we will live with strength.

Because change causes us grief, inflexible people think differently to flexible people. Inflexible people set up deflective mechanisms in their thinking, so they don't have to change.

I cheekily wrote a blog about the way inflexible people think. They give defensive names to others whose lifestyles of devotion threaten their routine. Here's my list:

Fanatic – Anyone more dedicated than you.
Hype – Any news that makes you feel inadequate.
Workaholic – Those who get to work before you.
Lazy – Those who get to work after you.
Immature – Anyone having more fun than you.
Prosperity Preacher – People who claim God gives them things.

Heretic – Anyone saying anything you've not heard before.

Extremist – People who get excited in worship.

Head in the Clouds – Anyone who prays more than you.

Old Fashioned – People who believe in repentance & sin.

Exaggeration – Stories of miracles.

Flake – Anyone who claims to have experienced supernatural phenomenon.

Too Good to be True – Anything relating to faith, grace or God's goodness.

Unscriptural – Anyone/anything you want! You can find a verse for most things and most don't know the Bible well enough to fight you on it!

O.T.T. (Over The Top!) – Anyone who behaves like those listed in Hebrews 11.

Eccentric – People who do the kind of stuff Jesus did.

The inflexible keep putting up walls to avoid change, but eventually change gets us all. When change finally comes and breaks into the world of the brittle, it comes with great trauma, as the world they have tried to hold in place falls apart around them.

Much better to be a "righteous palm," bending to God's winds of change, leaning in to the lessons of life, stretching to grow through every experience that God brings. That way you will be strong for every season of your life.

For Group Discussion:

1. Would you describe yourself as flexible, or do you struggle with change?

2. Why do you think some people struggle more with change and flexibility than others?

3. How can you develop a more flexible attitude and mind-set?

4. Why do you think flexibility is important to spirituality and destiny?

Chapter Five: Building A Firm Foundation

"Do not despise the day of small beginnings" Zechariah 4:10

Famed preacher Leonard Ravenhill wrote about a group of tourists visiting a picturesque village, who walked by an old man sitting beside a fence. In a rather patronizing way, one tourist asked, "Were any great men born in this village?" The old man replied, "Nope, only babies."

Everyone starts somewhere. Usually it's in a small, hidden, forming, developing place. Like a building with hidden foundations, you must go through a foundational stage to build a strong life.

In Matthew chapter 7 Jesus ends his famous "sermon on the mount" with these words:

"Therefore everyone who hears these words of mine and puts them into practice is like a wise man who built his house on the rock. The rain came down, the streams rose, and the winds blew and beat against that house; yet it did not fall, because it had its foundation on the rock. But everyone who hears these words of mine and does not put them into practice is like a foolish man who

built his house on sand. The rain came down, the streams rose, and the winds blew and beat against that house, and it fell with a great crash."

Getting your foundation right is one of the most vital parts of living strong.

But I don't know about you, foundations don't seem too 'sexy'! They are not fun, cool or initially rewarding. People don't come to see your new house and say "Ooo nice foundation!"

It's all hidden stuff, it's dirt, and once the building is up, you don't ever sit admiring the foundation – you can't even see them! Yet the building won't stand if it's not there.

Jesus says your life has exactly the same principles as a tall building or a house. You've got to build and dig right into foundation issues, to go through some real processes, if you want to build a life that can withstand the storms that will come.

If You've Got A Crooked Foundation, You Will Build A Crooked House

There's no way you can avoid this truth. Faulty foundations make for faulty houses. When the rains of either hard times or success come, your house is going to be tested so you need to get the foundation right. (Don't be scared by that – that's why we're going on this journey together! Stick with me…)

I love the fact that this scripture speaks of building a house. To me, that is the reality that you are not building only for yourself, but for your children, and for your children's children.

Look at the effect of a good foundation in one man's life -

An investigation into the famed 18th century revival preacher Jonathan Edwards (1703-58) showed that, of the 1,394 known descendants of Jonathan Edwards, 100 became preachers and missionaries, 100 lawyers, 80 public officials, 75 army and navy officers, 65 college professors, 60 physicians, 60 prominent authors, 30 judges, 13 college presidents, 3 United States senators, and one a vice-president of the United States.

Compare him with another man of that era, Max Jukes. Mr Jukes had 310 descendants who died as paupers, 150 were criminals, 100 were drunkards, 7 were murderers, and more than half of the women were prostitutes. *

Wow! Your foundation is going to affect GENERATIONS to come.

When you build a strong foundation, you are building for your children, and their children, and their children's children!

Your attitude to divorce, alcohol, sexual sin, money, leadership, fear, God, anger, mental health, greed, materialism, pride, humility, authority, prayer will probably rattle right through generations after you, for no other reason than people will be brought up in families that consider a certain "way" to be normal and right. Very few will dig right into the foundations of how a man, or a family, think – and confront and confess issues. So both weaknesses and strengths often last for generations in a family line.

Very few that is, except you. You, like me, want to journey right into our foundations with God's powerful grace. We could be the generation that changes our family's weaknesses into strengths! It could be YOU that ends the cycle of divorce, of fatherlessness, of debt, of addiction, of fear. It could be YOU that turns the next 20 generations of your family into church goers, nation changers and devoted fathers.

It could be you. If you will dig deep.

How God Builds Foundations

There is a part to foundation building that is really simple – it's about a cleansing work in your heart whilst you are hidden.

"Then he went down to Nazareth with them and was obedient to them. But His mother treasured all these things in her heart. And Jesus grew in wisdom and stature, and in favour with God and man." Luke 2:51-52

Jesus had about 17 years of His life when all we know about Him is He "grew in wisdom and stature and favour with God and man." In other words, He was growing up. As a man. In His character. As someone who could relate to God (That's favour with God) and He was learning how to relate to people (That's favour with man). He was hidden and all was pretty mundane and quiet as far as we can see. Some call it "The Silent Years" – when all of life gets summed up in just a verse or two.

You should experience silent years too. They build strength in you. Times when you're just learning how to be a man, or woman. How to relate to God. How to relate to others. It's your foundation.

Isaiah 49 spoke of it this way:

"Listen to me, you islands; hear this, you distant nations:
Before I was born the LORD called me; from my mother's womb He has spoken my name.
He made my mouth like a sharpened sword, in the shadow of His hand He hid me;
He made me into a polished arrow and concealed me in his quiver.
He said to me, "You are my servant, Israel, in whom I will display my splendour."
But I said, "I have laboured in vain; I have spent my strength for nothing at all.

Yet what is due me is in the LORD's hand, and my reward is with my God."

Even Jesus needed to be hidden in that quiver for a season.

Now, that will be frustrating to people like me, and perhaps you. People who are driven, ambitious (even in a good way), who want to make their mark and get on with "destiny" don't like the idea of apparent unproductiveness– but this is an important part of destiny.

We will all go through seasons when we feel hidden, to the point where we will wonder with Isaiah, "I have laboured in vain; I have spent my strength for nothing at all."

But you see, there are some things that only "being hidden" will do. James 1:4 says, *"Let perseverance do it's perfect (or maturing) work."* There are some foundational things that only waiting, patience, hiddenness, being overlooked and forgotten will do.

There are issues of pride, approval, value and sonship that are only learned in the darkness of a quiver, waiting to be used. (It's an active kind of waiting, though – Jesus had wardrobes to build and things to learn!)

At age 18 I wanted to change the world, to be the next man of God! But in truth, I was an idiot! My greatest disadvantage is that I did not know what I did not know, which was dangerous.

Now I've had great fun, good friends and favoured times all through my life, but I do know that in many ways God "quivered" me – hid me, set tight boundaries around me. Stopped me from doing some things I would have liked to do. He stopped me trying to fast track into my future, and let me go the good long route. He allowed "due process" so I would be strong enough for a long, fruitful life with Him.

Learning To Live Right

A lot of our foundational years are about learning to do right when there's no great applause, sometimes even little fruit. Notice the wise man in Jesus' parable was the one who "put these words into practice." Building a foundation is about learning to do right in the dark. Serve right. Love right. Talk right. Spend right. Think right.

There is no way to fast track and avoid building your foundation. If you do, by running from learning, humility, obscurity or avoiding serving others, you will pay the price later. You don't have to look far to find Christians who love God, but their practices have led to failed marriages, debt, shamed ministries and broken homes. Weaknesses in their foundations, eventually catch up with them, and their crooked houses fall.

But the results are beautiful if you let God build a strong foundation in your life. The "quivered" prophecy goes on to say in Isaiah:

"And now the LORD says — He who formed me in the womb to be his servant
to bring Jacob back to Him and gather Israel to Himself,
for I am honoured in the eyes of the LORD and my God has been my strength—
He says: "It is too small a thing for you to be my servant
to restore the tribes of Jacob and bring back those of Israel I have kept.
I will also make you a light for the Gentiles,
that my salvation may reach to the ends of the earth."

For Group Discussion:

1. Why is it important to build a solid foundation to your life? What might this mean?

2. Can anyone describe foundational issues in generations of families, personal or theoretical, that could be solved by someone re-digging the foundations, and growing in biblical truth?

3. Foundations are often about hidden development. What do you think hiddenness looks like? How might being hidden cause someone to grow in strength? Can anyone describe going through this and how it developed them?

Chapter Six: The Power Of Your Thoughts

"As a man thinks, so is he." Proverbs 23:7

Here is a profound lesson for life: You cannot change your behaviour without changing your thoughts.

Thoughts are the channels through which your personal power, actions, words and even the activities of heaven will flow.

"Do not conform to the pattern of this world, but be transformed by the renewing of your mind." Romans 12:2

Here Paul's letter to the Romans tells us that we can be utterly transformed, literally meaning a metamorphosis will take place, like when a caterpillar becomes a butterfly, if we renew our minds.

Many of us may draw close to God in our hearts, love Him in our worship, desire Him with our longings and are attracted to Him with our desires – and yet our lives do not radically alter! Sometimes we can even feel and sense His tremendous power filling our lives, and still we sin addictively, perform few or no miracles, walk in poor confidence and back away from challenges. Why is this?

It is because there is a law at work inside you, which says, "As a man thinks, so is he."

You will be as strong as your thought-life. As powerful as your thinking. As confident as your mindset. As mighty as your mental processes.

This law means that I know of many perfectly capable people who think themselves incapable – and guess what, they go on to live irrelevant lives! I know lovely men who think themselves to be poor fathers – sure enough, they eventually become what they think themselves to be and destroy their families.

Fear, insecurity, suspicion, worry, poor self image, self-obsession, addiction to the approval of others – all these work inside us to shorten our stride, steal our confidence, put us off course, miss divine appointments and ultimately shipwreck our entire destiny.

You must change your mind, to begin to think as God thinks, in order to live a godly destiny.

"For my thoughts are not your thoughts, neither are your ways my ways," declares the LORD. "As the heavens are higher than the earth, so are my ways higher than your ways, and my thoughts than your thoughts." Isaiah 55:8-9.

God doesn't think like us, His thoughts are SO much higher! As Smith Wiggleworth puts it, "If we want to do as Jesus did, we must first think as Jesus thought." We need to upgrade our thinking, to enter the fullness of life promised by Jesus.

Well-Trodden Neural Pathways
Your brain is a mass of Neural Pathways - actual, biological paths, created by you through repetitive thought, action and behaviours. These develop and become extremely powerful.

It is because of these pathways that we can walk around our house in the dark and not hit furniture, as we're so used to the layout in our minds. You may sometimes drive to work and realise you can't remember 3 miles of it, as you did it subconsciously. (Dangerous, I might add!) You wash in the shower in a certain way each morning, shave a certain way.

Your brain creates pathways, so that what starts as conscious behaviour, soon becomes sub-conscious and completely automatic.

Now, it means little when we talk of showering or shaving – but we also create pathways in response to belief, life, attitudes and ministry. We create pathways of worry, anxiety, fear, or of faith, boldness and trust, by repeated responses, thoughts and actions.

Sometimes an area in our lives becomes particularly powerfully trained in a negative subconscious way – (The Bible calls this a 'Stronghold' in 2 Corinthians 10:4) and we find it hard to rewire.

Perhaps we build a stronghold of worry over finance for years, and we unintentionally teach ourselves to panic when the bills mount up. The first few times it is conscious worry and stress. But as the years roll on, in the end, when that bill hits the doormat, your subconscious mind heads off down the path of worry, before you've had a moment to pray and trust God!

It's as though your thoughts say, "We know what to do when this happens, let's go" and off your mind goes, sprinting down the path of panic. So now you define yourself as a worrier about finance.

Well, actually, you just used the powerful law of thoughts to MAKE yourself a worrier!

You see, the mind is a great servant, but a poor master. You must renew it and have it serve your heart well.

Perhaps it's not money, perhaps it's sickness; just one pain and your mind runs down the path of panic, worrying that it's cancer.

"This is it!" Your mind tells you, "The big one … I knew it would happen eventually!"

Perhaps it's lust, anger, insecurity, fear, a self-image issue, shame – you've spent years laying a path and now you are well trained to sub-consciously take that path when a trigger is hit – and now it has become "part of you" – there's nothing you can to. Or is there…?

The Pathways Of The Mind
Jesus spoke of pathways in the parable of the sower.

In Mark 4:3 Jesus says, *"A farmer went out to sow his seed. As He was scattering the seed, some fell along the path, and the birds came and ate it up."* The sower then went on to sow on the rocky places, the thorns and the good soil.

In explaining the parable, Jesus said, *"The secret of the kingdom of God has been given to you…. The farmer sows the word. Some people are like seed along the path, where the word is sown. As soon as they hear it, Satan comes and takes away the word that was sown in them."*

He then explains that the farmer, (God) is sowing seed (the Word), along hard pathways in our lives. But the seed can't penetrate the pathways. The result is that the enemy can simply come along and take the Word of God away.

Jesus is teaching that we have pathways in our minds, which are so well trodden, the Word of God never takes root. Pathways of panic, or fear over money, poor mind-sets regarding health, destiny, relationships, conflict or identity.

We might say an 'Amen!' in the meeting when we hear it, and feel a flicker of "That's how I want to think and live." But these paths are so well trodden in our thinking, that by the time we're leaving the church building, we're talking like an atheist again! Fears arise easily and by the time Monday arrives, we're back to old thoughts of worry, stress, fear and it is as though our minds are completely untouched by the word of God!

In the areas where we have developed well-walked pathways, we need to "break up the unploughed ground!" (Hosea 10:12) We need to have an overhaul in our thinking. We need to ask God to help us renew our minds; otherwise we will live trapped in patterns of behaviour that are hard to break.

Renewing The Mind

Romans 10:17 says, *"Faith comes by hearing the word."* It is actually a continuous tense which means *"Faith comes by hearing and hearing and hearing…"*

To reconstruct our thinking we need to start digging at the roots of our stinking thinking, not merely by a single message from the preacher at church once a week, but by digging into the promises of the Bible daily. We need to read faith-filled books specifically about our weak areas of thinking. Listen to podcasts. Write some scriptures on post-it notes and litter your house with them.

Meditation

Biblical meditation is one of the ways we overhaul our minds. This has nothing to do with emptying our minds, like eastern mystical meditation. This is about filling our minds with the Word of God.

God spoke to Joshua as he was about to start leading the Children of Israel into a new stage of destiny:

"Do not let this Book of the Law depart from your mouth; meditate on it day and night, so that you may be careful to do everything written in it. Then you will be prosperous and successful." Joshua 1:8

God told Joshua to meditate on the scriptures "to make his ways successful."

Of course, to make his outer way successful he needed to first make his "thought pathways" successful, because "As a man thinks, so is he."

So God said "Do not let this Book of the Law depart from your mouth." Please note, God said to speak it, to put it in his mouth, not simply inwardly think it over.

You see, we enter things into our minds by our speech and our imagination. Phil Pringle uses the illustration that our mouths are a keyboard, and our brains like a computer. We input into a computer with a keyboard, and we input into our minds, by our mouths.

"The tongue has the power of life and death, and those who love it will eat its fruit." Proverbs 18:21

Speech and visualisation is how we update the powerful software of our minds, in God. Speech is incredibly powerful in reprogramming our minds and so Biblical, Jewish meditation, actually talks about "mumbling" and "repeating" phrases to help get them into our minds, hearts and spirits.

Can you imagine if every time you had a poor quality thought about God's provision, you mumbled, "It is written: God is my Provider." If you countered every worry about sickness with, "By His wounds I am healed!" If you fought every fear with "God has not given me a spirit of fear!"

Now, you cannot think one thing, and say another simultaneously (try it!). If, in this way, you started to take every stinking, poor thought captive, and make it obedient to Christ's way of thinking, then those strongholds would begin to fall.

The result is that you would begin to think as God thinks. Then, in communion with Him, you would start to do what God does! Life would become very powerful indeed!

What You Focus On Grows

Finally, a great principle of how your mind works is to understand that what you focus on, will grow.

What you feed becomes strong.

What you starve becomes weak.

Intensively starve fears of focus, time and energy and those fears will begin to diminish. Replace fear thoughts with a mumbling confession of God's truth, protection and love for you and you will be digging over that pathway and creating a new one.

Starve hypochondria. Stop meditating on being sick! Stop worrying. Read the Bible, get some confession stickers around your house, refuse to waste emotional energy on it.

"Finally, brothers and sisters, whatever is true, whatever is noble, whatever is right, whatever is pure, whatever is lovely, whatever is admirable—if anything is excellent or praiseworthy—think about such things. Whatever you have learned or received or heard from me, or seen in me—put it into practice. And the God of peace will be with you." Philippians 4:8

Focus on health, life, grace, mercy, others, God Himself. Make your mind think about Bible verses, pop on worship music (I sometimes play worship music 24 hours a day when I'm working on an area of my mind!), be around people that re-enforce God's thoughts in you – people of faith.

As your thoughts line up with His, you will not simply feel God's presence and power, but learn how to release it into your world in powerful ways.

Dr. Stanley E Jones wrote, *"I am inwardly fashioned for faith, not for fear. Fear is not my native land; faith is. I am so made that worry and anxiety are sand in the machinery of life; faith is the oil. I live better by faith and confidence than by fear, doubt and anxiety. In anxiety and worry, my being is gasping for breath— these are not my native air. But in faith and confidence, I breathe freely—these are my native air.*

A John Hopkins University doctor says, "We do not know why it is that worriers die sooner than the non-worriers, but that is a fact." But I, who am simple of mind, think I know; We are inwardly constructed in nerve and tissue, brain cell and soul, for faith and not for fear. God made us that way. To live by worry is to live against reality."

As you plough up weak thought patterns of fear, worry, lust or anger, and replace them with divine thoughts of love, peace, joy and faith, you're going to find strength pours through your soul. You will start to live at peace with God, with yourself and with others.

That is a strong way to live.

For Group Discussion:

1. "As a man thinks, so is he" Proverbs 23:7. Discuss why this verse is so profound.

2. Your brain is a mass of neural pathways. What things do you do repeatedly, with little thought of conscious reasoning?

3. Read the Dr. Stanley E Jones quote, just before the end of this chapter. Discuss its truths.

4. Are there practical things you can do, to help you renew your mind, and to begin to think like God thinks? Discuss.

Chapter Seven:
Embarrass Sin Before It Embarrasses You!

"One leak will sink a ship, and one sin will destroy a sinner."
John Bunyan

A Pastor had a woman in his congregation who was a pain. She constantly criticised his sermons, poked fun at his bald patch, objected to his projects and slandered him to her friends.

As weeks turned to months this woman really got under his skin. He found himself thinking about the things she'd said, letters she'd written, jibes she'd pointed at him, and he was starting to get bitter. Irritated and bitter.

As the months rolled on his bitterness turned to anger, but he didn't quite know what to do about it. He was, if he was honest, really starting to actually hate this woman. Here he was, a Pastor, hating one of his congregation members!

One day he was driving to town, approaching a slow long curve in the road. Suddenly he saw the woman coming towards him in her car. Her window was open and she leaned out and shouted at him -

"PIG!"

In an instant, all the bitterness, rage and hate shot out of him like a geyser, and he leaned his now red and veined, bald, angry head out of his car window and shouted back "YOU COW! COW! COW!"

Then he drove around the corner into the pig.

Sorry, that was a joke. A bad one.

But it kind of leads me into where I'm going with this vital ingredient to developing strength in our lives:

What Is In You, Will Eventually Come Out

Matthew 12:35 says, *"The good man brings good things out of the good stored up in him, and the evil man brings evil things out of the evil stored up in him."*

Whoever said, "You are what you eat" was right you know! Eventually, what is in you, placed there by harboured experiences, reactions, meditations, nature and nurture, it will all come out one day, when you are placed under pressure. When it comes out under violent pressure, if there's bad in you, it usually isn't pretty!

The word "brings" in Matthew 12:35 has a fuller meaning to it than we see in most Bibles. It hints at a violent bringing forth. Like a sponge violently squeezed, one day strong reactions will come shooting out, unable to be contained any longer.

Stored up lusts develop into adulterous affairs and pornographic addictions. Secret hidden alcoholic abuse will come out in poor mental health and soul destruction. Greed violently springs out as uncontrollable debt and selfishness, hate destroys relationships, hurt and shame destroys our emotional wellbeing. Fear traps us aggressively in disobedient, rebellious or passive behaviour.

Like the pastor who stored up his bitter dislike of his congregation member, one day, when he least expected it, out poured his now full-grown hatred! He was so blinded he assumed the woman was once again castigating him, not warning him of a pig in the road!

James 1:15 tells us, *"... after desire has conceived, it gives birth to sin; and sin, when it is full-grown, gives birth to death."* Sin grows in us, starting as a hardly noticeable seed, until it completely destroys us.

In John Henry Jowett's 'The Grace Awakening' he writes, *"Sin is a blasting presence, and every fine power shrinks and withers in the destructive heat. Every spiritual delicacy succumbs to its malignant touch...Sin impairs the sight, and works toward blindness. Sin numbs the hearing and makes men deaf. Sin perverts the taste, causing men to confound the sweet with the bitter, and the bitter with the sweet. Sin hardens the touch, and eventually renders a man past feeling."*

There's Great Strength In Repentance

"Repent therefore...and turn to God...so that your sins may be wiped out and that times of refreshing may come from the presence of the Lord." Acts 3:19

Repentance will never, ever go out of fashion, this side of heaven. We will always need to turn back to God and ask Him to help us with angry thoughts, hurt emotions, lustful longings, greedy desires, selfish impulses and aggressive words. Sometimes it will be daily, even hourly, that we turn to heaven and say, "God forgive me, cleanse me, that's not how I want to live!"

But if you store it, instead of offering it before God for cleansing, it will come back to weaken you, often with destiny altering consequences.

Defining Sin

"There is a class of people who are pure in their own eyes, and yet

are not washed from their own filth." (Proverbs 30:12 AMP)

It would seem, that as cultures change and times move, our perceptions of what is sin might change. But the truth is "God changes not" (Malachi 3:6). Sin will always be sin.

It has always been wrong, and is wrong today, to lust, be hateful, steal, be greedy, selfish, or to worship any other god. I heard idolatry brilliantly defined as "Whatever you need to ask permission from, before you obey God." Wow!

The danger is we dilute our perception of sin over time, and so our reaction to sin slowly changes.

We subtly give in to hatred, as we defend and justify the fact that someone has hurt us. We allow a creeping lust through imaginings and daydreams, until we subtly think pornography is acceptable (I'm not harming anyone, we think). We subtly drink to increasing excess (Well He did turn water into wine, we say). We are cruel in our words, calling on righteous judgement as our defence for hateful comments. We gossip, under the guise of "prayer requests."

Slowly, subtly, sin creeps up on us.

But repentance and confession to God is still the turning point from condemnation, and baptises us into the ocean of God's amazing grace – the power to live above sin.

So how do we deal with sin, it's power, it's very real destructive and deceptive qualities?

Don't Dilute Your Reaction To Sin
I love the quote *"Embarrass sin before it embarrasses you."*

I heard of a preacher who was on an airplane flight and the woman sat next to him tried to subtly make a 'pass' at him. Once he realised what was going on he stood to his feet and, in front of all the other passengers, pointed at the woman and loudly announced, "Harlot of Babylon! She's a harlot of Babylon!" Ha!

A tad over the top I suppose, but you get the picture. When sin comes knocking, don't sit, ponder, wonder, play with the thought, the environment or the idea for a moment. No, REACT FAST!

When Potiphar's wife made a pass at Joseph in Genesis 39:12 he RAN! Run from sin! Don't start thinking, "I wonder if I'm strong enough to endure it for a bit?" ...that's a deception. It's also dumb.

I heard one teacher talk about the 'spit reaction'. If you get a fly in your mouth you spit, straight away. You don't taste it for a bit, wash it around in your mouth. No, you spit!

As soon as sin, be it anger, hurt, lust, an area of addiction, greed or compromise comes knocking...spit it out, straight away. Then call on God to help you!

With lust, particularly in men, it's been proven you have about one minute of pondering anywhere close to a lustful thought, before all the chemical reactions of your body are going to kick in wanting sex. You have less than a minute to say, "I'm out of here" before you are getting past the point of no return. Get out, run, take a cold shower, go for a walk, start to worship!

Remember the olden days when internet images would load slowly, unwinding from bottom to top? I was in my office, my staff all working next door, and I had clicked on a link on the internet, harmlessly checking something out. The page I clicked on slowly started to load from the bottom. I couldn't quite make out the picture so I tilted my head to the side. I squinted. I tilted to the other side. I couldn't quite make it out. A bit more loaded, then more scrolled. Slowly my mind grasped what I was studying so intently. It was a pair of breasts!

What I did next pleased me…

"BOOBIES!" I exclaimed…"I CAN SEE BOOBIES!!" About 5 staff turned and looked up from their desks next door; wide eyed they stared at me through the large glass window that separated us, then burst into laughter at their mad leader!

Something that could have thrown temptation my way, instead became a moment of hysterical amusement, as my staff all laughed. They knew what I was doing:

I was embarrassing sin, before it embarrassed me.

Even now, when I preach my 'Boobies' sermon, it is one of my more memorable ones. (Though I don't use a PowerPoint presentation for that one…ahem.)

Feed Your Spirit-Man
"Do not be deceived: God cannot be mocked. A man reaps what he sows. Whoever sows to please their flesh, from the flesh will reap destruction; whoever sows to please the Spirit, from the Spirit will reap eternal life." Galatians 6:7-8

There is a fight between Spirit and flesh going on in us all.

My dad always used to teach that it is as though there are two dogs having a fight for your soul. You ask me, "Which one is going to win?" The dog that you feed, is the dog that will win.

Live to feed the flesh with greed, lust, anger, hate, dwell on hurts and meditate on fears and that is who you will be. You simply make it more and more powerful by thinking on such things.

But, if you repent, turn and feed yourself on goodness, kindness, purity, love, selfless thoughts backed up by selfless actions, you will keep empowering the spirit-man in you, and eventually, more and more, you will become strong in God. If you keep running to

God and from sin-provoking circumstances, the sinful dog will weaken.

Truly, an addictive sin-stronghold that you think is mighty and unconquerable today, will be a weakened skeletal wimp in three months, if you feed the "good-dog" in you! Fill your heart with good things, run from the sin, and you will become mighty in the grace and strength of God.

For Group Discussion:

1. Discuss why repentance, (meaning, to turn from sin) is so important.
2. What was once considered sinful in society, may now be accepted or even celebrated. How is this dangerous?
3. How can we embarrass sin, before it embarrasses us?
4. How can we feed our spirit-man, and starve our sinful, flesh man?

Chapter Eight: Living in Your Grace Zone

"All men dream but not equally. Those who dream by night in the dusty recesses of their minds awake to the day to find it was all vanity. But the dreamers of the day are dangerous men, for they act out their dreams with open eyes, to make them possible..."
T.E. Lawrence

"Without a vision" Proverbs 29:18 says, *"we cast off restraint"* or perish. Vision, purpose or dreams bring restraint, discipline and focus to our lives. But we become weak, feeble, and useless when we fail to stick to the grace zone and vision God has ordained for our lives:

"Be strong in the grace that is in Christ Jesus." 2 Timothy 2:1

There is a kind of strength that comes from sticking to your grace zone, your calling, the place where God has designed you to operate.

The Strength Of Usefulness
There was a beautiful aqueduct that was hundreds of years old. It was stunning and brought water to a town for centuries. In modern

times, the locals decided to honour it by not using it anymore, and laying pipes instead. They wanted to honour the aqueduct by making it a monument. "We should put a plaque on it" they thought "and let it retire gracefully from its long service, so that it will never be forgotten."

But the very attempt to honour that aqueduct by ending its use, actually destroyed it.

Within a few months it began to crumble because water was not flowing through it anymore. You see, it was in its usefulness that it found strength. When the aqueduct was in its vision or grace zone, it was strong because it was doing what it was made to do. *

This is the same with you. You will be strong when you do what God made you to do.

King David, the warrior, decided not to go to war in the springtime. Instead of fighting his enemies, he decided to stay home and rest. But this is the very time when we find King David on a balcony, eyeing up a beautiful woman, and the weakest, most feeble season of his life begins. In the very moment he abdicated his reason for living, he became weak.

We know the rest of the story; he slept with her, they had a child, the child died, and in actual fact David's kingdom was never quite the same again. Though God forgave him and restored his relationship with God, his destiny was irretrievably altered.

There's a strength in doing what you were made to do.

How To Know Your Vision
Andy Stanley gives us one great way to discover our grace zone: Simply ask yourself the question, "When I am near the end of my life, what do I want a long line of people to thank me for?"

Once you can answer this question you will discover what is right at the core of your being. Perhaps you have a desire to alleviate poverty in some way, or to raise an extraordinary family, or to release finances into the kingdom of God. Perhaps you really desire to care for people and so you will be some sort of pastor or counsellor. Perhaps you want to show people the power and presence of God, and so you will live to reveal the Holy Spirit to people. Perhaps the greatest desire of your heart is to win as many souls to Jesus as possible, and so your primary passion is to be an evangelist? Maybe you love to teach, to train or to fiddle with technology or engineering?

Of course there are usually many parts to our dream, our call, and the purpose God has for us, but if we answer honestly we will often discover there is one thing that truly drives us.

Perhaps you haven't discovered that one thing yet? What should you do?

Quite simply, look at several factors: Firstly, what irritates you? What do you passionately want to change about the world?

Secondly, what excites you? What, when others are talking about it, makes your pulse slightly race?

Thirdly, what giftings have you got? What are you naturally good at? Do you love to support others in a dream or task? Are you administrative, creative, pastoral, hospitable, do you love to write, do you love to coach, do you love to support, are you good at spreadsheets and mathematics? I know for sure that last one is not me!

Lastly, listen to the voice of God. Get a notepad and a pen, set aside some time, and begin to write what you think God might be saying to you. It may come in feelings, impressions, single words that wash over your soul repeatedly, or an entire paragraph of detailed information. As you give space to listen to the still small voice of God, you will find He speaks (There is an entire chapter on 'Hearing God's Voice' in my book 'Glory in the Church').

As God speaks, He will show you your grace zone.

I remember in November 1990 God began to speak to me about my life. For several months, several hours a day, God put impressions, pictures of the future, dreams and whispers my way, and these all nudged me into my grace zone, where I could find strength.

If you look at what irritates you, what excites you, what you're naturally good at, and all that God has been speaking to you, and begin to develop in those things, you are going to discover your grace zone.

Go to your Pastors and ask them, "Can I get involved in this thing that excites me?" or "Can I help fix this thing that irritates me?" or "Can I try and use my gifting in this thing that I think I'm good at?" If you begin to get involved at church, at work, at home or in your community with these sorts of things, you will discover the very reason you were born.

It may be for a season that you need to try out quite a few areas of church, business or ministry life to discover your grace zone. Do it, chat to your Pastor, and go learn from all the great leaders around you, through practice, exploration and adventure, and in this way you'll find strength for the days ahead.

For Group Discussion:

1. When you are near the end of your life, what do you want a long line of people to thank you for? Discuss.

2. Thinking of your giftings, irritations, passions and God's word to you, can you identify your grace zone?

3. Someone once said, "There is no such thing as retirement in the Bible." How might the concept of retirement, or ceasing work, have a negative effect on our overall strength? Discuss the strength of usefulness.

4. Between now and when you next meet, take a notepad and pen, and spend some time writing what you think God would say to you about your purpose. Report back to the group next time.

Chapter Nine: Two Are Better

"Two are better than one." Ecclesiastes 4:9

There's a Spanish story of a father and son who had become estranged. The son's name was Paco, a common name in Spain.

The son ran away and the father set off to find him. He searched for months to no avail. Finally, in a last desperate attempt to find him, the father put an advertisement in a local newspaper. The ad read: "Dear Paco, meet me in front of this newspaper office at noon on Saturday. All is forgiven. I love you. Your Father."

On the Saturday in question, hundreds of 'Pacos' turned up, looking for forgiveness and love from their fathers.*

Our world is desperately lonely. Despite our ability to travel, our hyper-connected world, the immergence of social media and the advancement of science, there is an epidemic of loneliness that does more harm than any life debilitating disease.

"It is not good for man to be alone...." God said to himself in Genesis 2:18. You were not designed for solitary confinement,

(that is a punishment in a prison!) but for community.

In fact, community is a means by which you can receive divine favour and grace in your life. It is a means of finding strength.

I read a wonderful story about Jimmy Durante, one of the great entertainers of a generation ago. He was asked to be a part of a show for World War II veterans. He told them his schedule was very busy and he could afford only a few minutes, but if they wouldn't mind him doing one short monologue and immediately leaving for his next appointment, he would come. Of course, the show's director agreed happily. But when Jimmy got on stage, something interesting happened. He went through the short monologue and then stayed. The applause grew louder and louder and he kept staying. Pretty soon, he had been on fifteen, twenty, then thirty minutes. Finally he took a last bow and left the stage. Backstage someone stopped him and said, "I thought you had to go after a few minutes. What happened?"

Jimmy answered, "I did have to go, but I can show you the reason I stayed. You can see for yourself if you'll look down on the front row."

In the front row were two men, each of whom had lost an arm in the war. One had lost his right arm and the other had lost his left. Together, they were able to clap, and that's exactly what they were doing, loudly and cheerfully! *

You see, as the movie put it, somehow we do "complete" each other. You, me and God – together we are a cycle of favour and grace, helping, healing, lifting, caring and covering.

This is exactly what makes the concept of church a strength-giving one:

"So highly does the Lord esteem the communion of His church,"

Calvin wrote, "that He considers everyone a traitor and apostate from religion who perversely withdraws himself from any Christian society which preserves the true ministry of the word and sacraments."

Psalm 92:12 says, *"The righteous will THRIVE like a palm tree, planted in the house of the Lord."* To be planted you need to allow your roots to go down deep into real friendships in a church setting. Do you have real, close friends in your church family? If not, then now is the time to dig in deeper, to find the strength of community.

You can do this by joining a small group or being in a small team, rather than simply turning up to larger meetings. While I love large worship services, I also love meeting with my small team to eat, laugh, talk and pray together. It's not enough for me to be in large meetings – I have to let myself be rooted.

In our church we call it living life "in circles."

Life In Circles

Life is better lived in circles than rows. Crowds who meet in rows facing the front of auditoriums have to move beyond that, to become friends around meal tables. Rows are not enough – everyone has to be in a circle.

It's how we are designed to be rooted.

I heard someone say, "People don't want to go to a friendly church – they want friends." In other words, it's about real friendships, not just bigger smiles from church stewards or organised pastoral care. We need to take time to build some friendships, and we will thrive!

But being rooted in godly friendships in God's House isn't always easy, I know! There are people that irritate me, frustrate me, or intimidate me, and it all takes time, and who has lots of time? Not me!

But I MUST make time to go deep into friendship with a few people because it makes me strong.

The Life In Dark Places

If a seed is to come to life, if it is to develop roots so it can grow and bear fruit, it has to go down into the damp darkness of soil, and trust that life will flow from that uncomfortable place.

It's the same in friendships and church. You have to be willing to go DEEP with a few people. To get uncomfortable. To take off the mask, get through the shallow "veneer" of new relationships, and go deep into some dark realities where great friends are made.

But you've got to trust that out of this uncomfortable place, where people are getting to know the real me, where I make an effort to spend time with people, before it ever starts to feel fun or rewarding – you've got to trust that life will start to flow from that place.

Suddenly, in the uncomfortable darkness of real relationships, you're going to find trust, forgiveness, laughter, peace, kind words, restoration, good advice and good grace starts to flow. You're thriving, planted in the house of the Lord!

Be brave. Stop just attending church services. Go deep, and make some friends for life. You're going to find strength flows from them, and you will also bring strength to them!

Eat Together

One great little secret I've learned in recent years is that we need to eat together with others.

I am being utterly serious here – I think there is a law of heaven, a grace-giving sacrament in eating together.

You see Jesus was really into food. Ever thought about that?

He started His ministry at a wedding feast, and ended it with the Last Supper. When He appears to His disciples, at one point He's making breakfast on the beach for them, on another occasion He asks them for something to eat.

Of course, Jesus will come back for us one day. We will rise and be with Him in heaven. Can you guess what He is going to say? You guessed it...He will say "LET'S EAT!" Then the Marriage Supper of the Lamb will begin!

Acts 2:46-47 shows us how the early church, a people living in a glorious revival, spent their days: *"They broke bread in their homes and ate together with glad and sincere hearts, praising God and enjoying the favour of all the people."*

I honestly believe that when we eat together, our love for each other deepens.

With my own staff and team, I had for a long time found things to be a little disconnected and overly task orientated, until I came across this little secret of eating together. We started to eat weekly, and also started to encourage all our teams, small groups and leaders to eat together more often – and the result was amazing. People started to talk about more than the latest deadline, or the current task – instead they began to enjoy each other! Asking about hopes, dreams, life, kids, sickness, sadness or holidays – the depth of relationship significantly increased and so too has our strength.

Eating together, in Jewish culture, is a deep sign of friendship and hospitality. Perhaps we too, should practice this life giving law of heaven, and we will find strength through friendships for years to come.

Go on, ask someone out to lunch right now. Start the journey!

Flying In Formation

Chuck Swindoll writes, "It's those stately geese I find especially impressive. Winging their way to a warmer climate, they often cover thousands of miles before reaching their destination. Have you ever studied why they fly as they do? It is fascinating to read what has been discovered about their flight pattern as well as their in-flight habits.

Four come to mind:

1. Those in front rotate their leadership. When one lead goose gets tired, it changes places with one in the wing of the V-formation and another flies point.

2. By flying as they do, the members of the flock create an upward air current for one another. Each flap of the wings literally creates an uplift for the bird immediately following. One author states that by flying in a V-formation, the whole flock gets 71 percent greater flying range than if each goose flew on its own.

3. When one goose gets sick or wounded, two fall out of formation with it and follow it down to help and protect it. They stay with the struggler until it's able to fly again.

4. The geese in the rear of the formation are the ones who do the honking. I suppose it's their way of announcing that they're following and that all is well. The repeated honks encourage those in front to stay at it.

As I think about all this, one lesson stands out above all others: it is the natural instinct of geese to work together. Whether it's rotating, flapping, helping, or simply honking, the flock is in it together...which enables them to accomplish what they set out to do."

There is strength to be found in flying in formation, together. To be caring, following, leading, eating, supporting, adventuring, fighting – together.

The book of Ephesians tells us we will rise to the full stature of Christ, as we are "built together" (Ephesians 2:22 & 4:15-16). It also shows us that in being built together, the sense of the Spirit of God will increase among us. Psalms 133 tells us that unity releases heaven's blessing. 1 Corinthians shows us the moving of God's Spirit is dependent on the whole body flowing together with him. It's pretty well cover to cover across God's word, that together we can be immensely powerful. That must be why our enemy is constantly trying to distract us into disunity through offence and insecurity. Fight it, go deep into friendships, let love conquer your fears and your independent spirit – and you will find strength.

For Group Discussion:

1. Our world is desperately lonely. Despite our ability to travel, our hyper-connected world, the immergence of social media and the advancement of science, there is an epidemic of loneliness that does more harm than any life debilitating disease. Discuss.

2. Community is a means by which we can receive divine favour and grace for our lives. It is a means of finding strength. What are the elements of community, that make it so powerful?

3. Proverbs 13:20 says, "He who walks with the wise grows wise, but a friend of fools suffers harm." Not all friendships are good; only correct, healthy friendships. How can you discern who is good for you, and develop a healthy friendship circle?

4. Why are deep relationships so hard to develop? But why is it worth the time and effort?

Chapter Ten: Skill Magnifies Strength

"Skill is better than strength" Polish Proverb

I love the TV show, 'World's Strongest Man.' I love to see them competing, running, carrying, pulling, stretching, fighting! One of my favourite events ever was an arm wrestling trial.

Firstly, on walked this huge man the size of a small house. He lumbered up to the podium to get ready to arm wrestle. From the other side of the arena walked a much smaller man. Instantly I thought this guy was going to get beaten easily. The smaller man walked up to the podium and faced the snarling bus sized figure in front of him, yet there wasn't an ounce of intimidation in the smaller man.

You see, the smaller man was the current world champion at arm wrestling. He wasn't as big, but he had better skills, and he knew it.

The two men got into position, clasped hands and braced themselves ready to wrestle. The countdown rang out; three, two, one ... and with a loud grunt they began to compete.

At first it just seemed as though the arms were locked stationary and would never move! As the seconds went on, the bigger man began to look more and more amazed that he wasn't instantly beating the smaller man.

10 seconds became 20 seconds, and 20 seconds 30, and the bigger man began to sweat, snort, and turn salmon pink, the veins bulging in his neck and forehead. His snorts turned to growls, as ripples of frustration began to stir in his chest. Still the smaller man stood his ground and held back the onslaught of this herd of muscle challenging him for his title.

When it seemed like the larger man was beginning to sense that he couldn't go on much longer, something rose up inside him, one final huge heave of muscle bound action, hoping that would break the deadlock. With a loud guttural scream he heaved and as he did, veins bulging, eyes protruding, teeth gnashing, you suddenly heard a loud crack.

Instantly there was a gasp in the crowd. The huge man stumbled back from the podium grasping his arm and crying out in pain.

He had broken his arm.

His muscles had tried to go somewhere his bones couldn't keep up.

You see, brute force is not the most important thing about strength. Sheer forcefulness is not what true strength is about. It's not about powering through because of the size of your bulk. There is more to strength than power.

The same is true of life. Strength in life is not just about the thickness of your skin, or how little it hurts when people are nasty to you. You would be wrong to think that true strength, godly strength, is about being pig-headed, thick-skinned and unstoppable.

Three Kinds Of Strength

Now sheer power is important in some ways, but there are three kinds of strength, naturally speaking, that enable your body to be truly strong. You need all three, and they present a great picture of your need to be strong in many ways, in order to be truly mighty:

Firstly, there is indeed physiological strength, which is your muscle size. You can grow your muscles by facing resistance. You can bulk up and become bigger, bolder, more confident and powerful.

But there are other kinds of strength too. There is neurological strength, the power of the signals to your muscles. It's the strength of your body to coordinate itself and to give instruction and to operate intelligently, sharply, skillfully.

Then there is mechanical strength, the strength of your joints. The strength of your body to cope with what is pushed against it. The flexibility of your body to cope with the strenuous things going on in your life.

In the same way life is not just about pure power and resilience, it's also about how you use the power you have. The smaller arm wrestler, who was a champion, beat the bigger man because of skill, because of posture, because of wisdom, because of intellect. He didn't just have strength, he knew how to use his strength, and maximise what he had, and it made him stronger than the "stronger" man! Get it?

The smaller man beat the larger man because of style. It was about technique, intelligence, skill.

The Unnecessary Battles Of Stupidity!

Many people are weakened in life because they foolishly think life is about brute "give me what I want" strength. Usually this means they end up in a lot of relational and organisational battles that they never needed to have. In turn, the battles weaken them, because they have lived without taking skill, or wisdom, into consideration, when thinking of strength.

As a church leader, people tell me all the time they have a marriage problem, or a money problem, or a relationship problem. After some discussion I usually discover they don't actually have a marriage problem or a money problem or relationship problem. What they actually have is a wisdom problem. A lack of wisdom is causing battles they don't even need to have. They are being destroyed by being dumb. Their foolishness is their failure. Their lack of regard for God's biblical advice, means they are fighting against God's ways, and weakening their chances of a blessed life.

The problem with fighting so many battles you don't need to have, by approaching life foolishly or without wisdom, is that the battles weaken you. Too much conflict will wear you out, exhaust you and burn you out.

But if we learn to maximise our strength through wisdom, skill, technique and godly intelligence then we will find we are able to live at full strength – because of "how" we are living.

The Benefits Of Skilfulness

If I had a room with 50 people in it, all willing to do something for God in a church setting, I know that there are leaders I could send into that room, that would share a vision, and come out with as many as 45 of those people ready to work on a team.

I also know that I have other leaders who are just as emotionally strong, just as spiritual, and perhaps even more prophetic than the first leader, and yet when they go into the room, they only managed to win over 15 people to work on their teams.

Why is that?

It's because life is so much more than brute strength. Life is also about skillful wisdom, learning favour with God and with man. It's about humility, Christ-likeness, kindness and interest in other people's lives.

Skilful Speech

Probably one of the greatest lessons of the book of Proverbs is how to use your tongue. Proverbs talks about teaching our lips, about learning how to speak. It talks about the power of life being in our tongues.

This means there is a skillfulness to talking, presenting ourselves, keeping ourselves from being hot-headed and over-reacting. There are gentle answers that can turn away anger, there are a healing words that can refresh others, there are ways of speaking that can bring us before kings and people of influence.

Simply by becoming skillful in speech, we can magnify the strength of our lives. We can reduce conflict, increase influence, heal relationships, and attract people to a purpose.

So don't just become more resilient, thick-skinned, or full of faith about your identity in Christ, also consider learning how to speak wisely.

Get Wisdom!

One definition of wisdom is "the correct application of truth." In other words, it's not just about knowing WHAT to do but HOW to do it. It's not just having a vision, it's knowing how God has designed you to fulfill that vision at maximum strength.

The book of Proverbs tells us of the value of wisdom:

"My son, if you accept my words and store up my commands within you, turning your ear to wisdom and applying your heart to understanding, and if you call out for insight and cry aloud for

understanding, and if you look for it as for silver and search for it as for hidden treasure, then you will understand the fear of the LORD and find the knowledge of God. For the LORD gives wisdom, and from his mouth come knowledge and understanding. He holds victory in store for the upright, he is a shield to those whose walk is blameless, for he guards the course of the just and protects the way of his faithful ones. Then you will understand what is right and just and fair - every good path. For wisdom will enter your heart, and knowledge will be pleasant to your soul. Discretion will protect you, and understanding will guard you."

Proverbs 2:1-11.

I love verse eight that says, *"He guards the course of the just and protects the way of His faithful ones."* Isn't that a picture of the strength that comes from seeking God's wisdom? If you accept His words, turn your ear, apply your heart, and treat God's wisdom as treasure, then you will enjoy victory, the shielding power of heaven, understanding, clarity and protection!

Invest In Your Skills & Wisdom

Go to some kind of Bible School, whether that's an evening class or on-line. Study the Bible. Read books about the language of healthy relationships. Take leadership courses and evaluations about how different people interact to the world, and learn how to lead yourself and others wisely. Learn about conflict resolution. Read the book of Proverbs. Study the lives of great leaders. Take a course in great leadership skills. Ask someone who has lived well for a coffee, and take some time to ask them questions about life, leadership, work, parenting, finances or health.

As you search out heavens wisdom, you are going to find all of heaven is backing up your actions, your words and your decisions – and that is a powerful way to live!

For Group Discussion:

1. How can wisdom help us be stronger?

2. How can wise words, be a powerful part of living a strong life?

3. How can you develop more wisdom and skills for life?

4. Think of three areas of your own life where it would be helpful to become wiser. What three people do you know who are excellent at one of these areas? Your assignment is to spend some time asking them questions about that area of their life.

Chapter Eleven: The Power Of Habit

"Motivation is what gets you started, habit is what keeps you going." Jim Rohn.

Proverbs 12:11 says, that *"He who chases fantasies will remain poor, but he who works his land will be rich."* Habit, or repeated action, is one way we empower our lives for strength by "working the land" of our lives. When our habits are good, we're going to be strong. When our habits are bad, weakness will prevail. If you don't know how to change poor habits for good, then you're forever at the mercy of ill-disciplined addictions. Creating great habits is part of living strong.

Someone once wrote, *"Excellence is not a singular act, but a habit. You are what you repeatedly do."*

There is something incredibly powerful in life when we discover the power of habit. Now I am a creative person, a prophetic person. I love to feel the moment and be spontaneous with what I'm doing in life.

But I've also discovered there is something incredibly powerful about habit, tradition, discipline and routine. There is something about developing a good pace in life, a great rhythm through healthy habits, that can make you strong.

A Steady Pace

When a runner runs, he doesn't want to constantly be changing his stride, or his pace. He will indeed change it from time to time, but only when he really needs to, because he knows there is strength in a steady pace. It conserves energy and gets his body into a sustainable rhythm.

This is also true in life. Charles Nobel said, *"First we make our habits, then our habits make us."* We must learn to have certain habits that make us strong and keep us strong.

Now we all have habits, from how much TV we watch and when we watch it, to habits with food - healthy food, and unhealthy food. We have leisure habits, exercise habits and "sit down and do nothing" habits! We have gossip habits, pity party habits, prayer habits and washing habits. Patterns that develop through the way we do life. Once ingrained, they are incredibly powerful. Therefore, we want to choose our habits, and not let our habits choose us!

Really strong people develop healthy habits. Habits for their prayer life, habits for their physical exercise, habits with their relationships, habits with their speech, their thoughts, their busy time and habits for their rest time. They have habits in their reading life, and habits in their friendship life and their married life. Little routines, ways of living that bring pace and stride to their 'run'. I think of these as little containers, windows of time, that we can fill with God moments and good moments, that all stir us on to live disciplined strong lives.

I Am Habit

I love this poem about the power of habit:

I am your constant companion.
I am your greatest helper or heaviest burden.
I will push you onward or drag you down to failure.
I am completely at your command
Half of the things you do you might as well turn over to me and I
will do them - quickly and correctly.
I am easily managed – but you must be firm with me.
Show me exactly how you want something done and after a few
lessons, I will do it automatically.
I am the servant of great people, and alas, of all failures as well.
Those who are great, I have made great.
Those who are failures, I have made failures.
I am not a machine though I work with the precision of a machine
plus the intelligence of a person.
You may run me for profit or run me for ruin - it makes no
difference to me.
Take me, train me, be firm with me, and I will place the world at
your feet.
Be easy with me and I will destroy you.
*Who am I? I am Habit.***

The Undisciplined despise themselves

Proverbs 15:32 says, *"Those who disregard discipline despise*
themselves."

I have always noticed that undisciplined people, who lack powerful
good habits, are generally unhappy with their lives. They can't
seem to find routine, pace, and do all the things they want to in
life.

Those who do not pray or develop a healthy prayer discipline, are
always aware that they are not living as they want to. Those who

do not eat well, rest well, enjoy friendships well or read the Bible well - these people are not living according to the pattern that God designed for us.

You cannot just run all guns blazing at life. You must have Sabbath days, prayer times, date nights, exercise and healthy mealtimes in order to live strong.

Energy Management

Energy management is more important than time management. We are all unique and have different energy levels, and different things that will either sap or increase our energy. We need to discover what replenishes or depletes us, and create habits accordingly.

While an extrovert may find other people replenishing, an introvert will find groups of people exhausting. Once we discover this we can build appropriate patterns of fellowship and solitude.

Personally, I need some quiet, solitude moments with God daily. I also need a couple of days' quiet preparation and prayer each week in order to do the public speaking I have to do. Then I need some thinking time to cope with the multiple decisions I make each day. I also need a couple of days with my team – but this can either replenish or exhaust me, depending on what we're having to face together! They are a great team, but if we are facing difficulty, even this can be tiring to an introvert like me.

I have come to know I also get energised by the sun (I grew up in the Mediterranean!), and by a bit of adventure. I get energised by "date time" with Vicky, my wife, and by playing with my son. I also get energised by sport, the Jacuzzi, writing, creativity and eating out!

On the other hand, I have learned that I get exhausted by groups of people I don't know, and that's OK (I am a little introverted here...I HATE parties!) I also get depleted by too many details, by conflict, (who doesn't?!) by spreadsheets, by too many mundane church meetings, (I go to A LOT!) or by too much time away from my family.

I have, at times, felt exhausted, weak, rung out and ratty in my job, but when I looked at my diary, it was obvious I was planning badly. I was in a high conflict resolution season, with loads of financial spreadsheets and too many party invitations in my diary! With little solitude time to compensate and too much travel away from my wife – my problem wasn't that I was weak; it was that I was unwise. I was planning badly.

These days I have learned to observe my life, know what will deplete me, and make sure I am mixing energy refueling habits in among my necessary energy depleting duties.

Finally, let's look at one of the most energising habits you can build into your life, a habit that empowers you whoever you are, whatever life you're living. To be truly strong in God, you need this habit:

The Prayer Habit

"But when you pray, go into your room, close the door and pray to your Father, who is unseen. Then your Father, who sees what is done in secret, will reward you… This, then, is how you should pray: "Our Father in heaven, hallowed be your name, your kingdom come, your will be done on earth as it is in heaven. Give us today our daily bread…" Matthew 6:6, 9,11.

Luke 5:16 tells, us that *"Jesus often withdrew to lonely places and prayed."*

In Matthew 6:9 Jesus tells us to pray by going into our rooms, closing the door, and praying to our Father, who, as some versions put it, is actually waiting for us in the "secret place" of prayer. It is in this place that we pray prayers like "Your kingdom come, Your will be done" and we draw God's strength into our lives.

Prayer is something Jesus teaches us we should do daily, as in verse 11 he teaches us to pray and ask God for that day's "bread," meaning that particular day's immediate needs.

Developing a daily prayer habit is one of the greatest things that will set apart the strong from the weak, and yet I do wonder if this incredible grace-giving habit is largely left undone by many? If, like most, you struggle with private prayer times, then I hope this wonderful story about developing a great daily habit in prayer inspires you.

The Chair

There was a Pastor in a church who wanted to teach his congregation about daily prayer. He taught one Sunday about having a daily moment with God in some way, so that you can build a strong life of intimacy with your Heavenly Father. He advised them to choose somewhere to pray that they would enjoy, and to add something pleasurable to their prayer lives, so that it would be enjoyable, and therefore, easily repeatable.

After the church service a businessman walked up to the Pastor irritated and red-faced. Angrily he said to the Pastor, "It's okay for you, you only work one day a week! I am a busy businessman, and I work long hours. How can I find time to pray, as well as run a business and be a husband and father. I do wish you'd stop making me feel guilty about this stuff!"

The Pastor paused for a moment and thought about what the man was saying, and replied, "I have always found that if you really want to do something in life, you will find a way to do it. If not, you will find an excuse. If you really want to pray, you will find a way to pray."

Well, that, of course, made the businessman even more angry, and he stomped off!

Several months later a man walked up to the Pastor at the end of the service, and said, "Do you remember me?" The Pastor looked at him, grasping for a name as many Pastors do with large congregations, and then it dawned on him; it was the businessman.

"You look completely different," said the Pastor.

"I sure am" replied the businessman

"What happened to you?" he asked.

"Well, I thought about what you said. You did annoy me, but after a while I did have to admit that you were right, if I really wanted to do something, I would find the time to do it. I'm a busy man, so I always have to find time to do the things I really want to do.

"So, I went home and I thought about what you said. You said that I should make prayer enjoyable, so that it's easily repeatable. I thought about this for a while and then remembered I've always wanted a rocking chair. So I got a rocking chair. I also love coffee, so I thought I could brew some fresh coffee and I'd only have to get up 15 minutes earlier in the morning to get 15 minutes with God.

"I also love my back garden, so I decided to get the rocking chair, and place it so it overlooks my back garden, and there, fresh coffee in hand, I started to read a little, listen a little, and give my concerns to God. It has completely transformed my life!"

Several months later the Pastor saw the man's wife at the end of a service and asked after her husband. "Hey, how's your husband doing with that rocking chair?"

"Oh my" exclaimed the wife, "He is a different man! That rocking chair has changed our marriage! Since he's been getting up half an hour earlier and spending time with God he is more centered, more attentive to me and closer to our children. That rocking chair has changed him."

Some months later the businessman came to see the Pastor and said, "Pastor, you know I spend 40 minutes every morning reading and praying on my rocking chair? (You noticed the length time growing yet?) Well, I just feel God's been saying to me for some weeks, that I need to go and help a Pastor friend in a new church plant in the next city. What you think?"

"Well you should spend some time listening to God and if you still feel the same in a few weeks, go for it!" the Pastor replied.

Several weeks later the businessman returned and still felt God was speaking to him about selling his business and helping this new church plant, so he did, and the new church prospered with his help.

Years later the man died and the Pastor travelled to the city where his family now lived, to console them and play a part at the funeral.

After the service, in the new widow's home, the Pastor spotted the rocking chair sat by a window overlooking a beautiful garden, coffee stained ring on the table nearby, next to a battered bible and journal.

"So what are you going to do with the rocking chair?" the Pastor asked the man's widow.

"Oh that rocking chair is going to stay in our family I hope" she replied. "It transformed my husband. He used to sit every morning, listening to God and reading the Bible. It made him a remarkable man. So I intend to pass that chair to my children in the hope that they would sit on the same chair that made their father a great man, and have their lives transformed in the same way. Perhaps my children will pass the chair to their children, so that generations of our family could be changed by a daily moment with God in the same way he was."

The Pastor wept at the simple, profound power, of creating a daily habit of encountering God. True strength in life comes not from any complex, unattainable ideal or idea. Power is very simple to find if we will just take the time to be with Him.

Where Is Your Chair?

So where is your daily habit of an encounter moment with God, His word, His voice?

Perhaps your "chair" is actually the habit of a walk by a river each morning, a certain seat in your favourite coffee shop, or a moment in a quiet room in your house with your favourite worship music playing?

Is it early in the morning or late at night? Is it on a long daily commute, with podcasts and teaching CDs, or just after the kids have gone to school, with a steaming cup of coffee, your favourite translation of the bible and a notepad to journal and doodle as you pray?

Did you notice that the man started with 15 minutes, but the time grew in the story as the years rolled on? You see, good habits become addictive, in all the right ways, and we start to truly feel the strength they bring.

When we develop a daily habit of prayer, it becomes a container that God can come and dwell in. It becomes a "chair we sit on," organised in our diary, a date in which we meet God and find strength.

Of course you'll talk to Him throughout your day, of course you'll hear His voice as you walk the streets, of course you're trying to be close as you go about your work, but you need quality time, built-in, routinely, so that you live a strong life. These organised habitual moments, anchor you into God's strength, so all the spontaneous "suddenlies" of God can happen more frequently.

Remember as we close this chapter on the strength found in habit, that Hebrews 11:6 tells us *"anyone who comes to Him must believe He exists and that He is a rewarder of those who diligently seek Him."*

I believe you will indeed be rewarded as you diligently seek God and live life with a healthy pace, habit and routine.

For Group Discussion:

1. What habits do you have, good or bad? What bad habits do you need to stop?

2. Why are good habits important?

3. Describe your prayer habits, good or bad (C'mon, be honest!) with the group.

4. How could you make your prayer habit better? "Make it enjoyable, so it's repeatable" the Pastor said. What could you add to your prayer life, to make it more enjoyable?

Chapter Twelve: Clothed With Strength

"The Sovereign Lord is my strength" Habakkuk 3:19

In 1577 St. Teresa of Avila, a Spanish Discalced Carmelite nun, wrote a book entitled "The Interior Castle." This fascinating work was about levels of intimate communion with God, and the powerful effect that will have upon a soul.

While obviously Catholic in theology, the title has fascinated me for some time: Can I build a strong interior castle within me through communion with God? Can a stronghold, a fortress of God's goodness, resilience and power, be constructed through intimate prayer? Can I be a temple for His Spirit, a conduit of His wisdom, a life flooded with His peace?

The strength that comes through a life focused on communion with God is not a new theme. King David wrote in the Psalms 27:4-6;

"One thing I ask from the LORD, this only do I seek: that I may dwell in the house of the LORD all the days of my life, to gaze on the beauty of the LORD and to seek Him in his temple. For in the day of trouble He will keep me safe in His dwelling; He will hide

me in the shelter of His sacred tent and set me high upon a rock. Then my head will be exalted above the enemies who surround me..."

Note that gazing leads to safety and salvation. As David communed with God, he expected strength to surround him. He repeats this theme most famously in Psalm 91:

"He who dwells in the shelter of the Most High will rest in the shadow of the Almighty. I will say of the LORD, "He is my refuge and my fortress, my God, in whom I trust." Surely He will save you from the fowler's snare and from the deadly pestilence. He will cover you with His feathers, and under His wings you will find refuge; His faithfulness will be your shield and rampart. You will not fear the terror of night, nor the arrow that flies by day, nor the pestilence that stalks in the darkness, nor the plague that destroys at midday. A thousand may fall at your side, ten thousand at your right hand, but it will not come near you." Psalm 91:1-7

In the 17th century Brother Lawrence wrote beautifully of "Practicing the Presence of God" – in short, finding inner peace and strength through a life of heart abandoned worship by focusing on God's love and care every moment of every day.

While Jesus' sacrificial death has won us the right to abide in God's most powerful presence, it would appear that a heart "set" on Him, is how we experience this incredible grace and access available to us through the cross. Many write that devoting our inner resources to meditation, day dreaming upon the divine and losing oneself in awe and tender devotion, leads to the opening of wells that pour heaven's grace into our broken humanity. Peace is found in habitually practicing the awareness of the Father's presence.

Head On A Pillow Peace

Mark 4:35-41 tells the story of Jesus calmly sleeping through a storm that terrified hardened fishermen:

"That day when evening came, He said to his disciples, "Let us go over to the other side." Leaving the crowd behind, they took Him along, just as He was, in the boat. There were also other boats with Him. A furious squall came up, and the waves broke over the boat, so that it was nearly swamped. Jesus was in the stern, sleeping on a cushion. The disciples woke Him and said to Him, "Teacher, don't you care if we drown?" He got up, rebuked the wind and said to the waves, "Quiet! Be still!" Then the wind died down and it was completely calm. He said to his disciples, "Why are you so afraid? Do you still have no faith?" They were terrified and asked each other, "Who is this? Even the wind and the waves obey Him!"

That "head on a pillow in every crisis" peace is what I want, how about you? To experience inner calm, whatever the circumstances.

I am too often thrown by conflict, illness, resistance or insecurity. Too often distracted by what is not truly valuable. If I'm being vulnerable and honest, I too often worship the god of the temporary, and take my eyes off the God of the Eternal. I too easily substitute the Everlasting Rock for the shifting sands of humanism. I replace worship with worry and praise with panic.

But I am slowly teaching my soul how to be anchored into the One who does not shift, whose word is immovable, whose promises are unchangeable, who is incapable of lying and will never grow weary. He can never be defeated, discouraged, despondent or disillusioned. His energy cannot run out, His wisdom will never be confused and His love for me will never waver.

He consistently covers my yesterdays in mercy, my today in grace and my tomorrows in hope. As I focus and the view of Him becomes clearer, I see it is not some light sprinkling of divine kindness that I had imagined He would give. No, when my heart is truly lost in Him I see His glory arrive on my shores like mighty, unconquerable ocean swells of unquenchable love. Like a raging sea breaking over my brokenness, breaching my weaknesses, invading my failure, and embracing my future with a beautiful, obsessive passion for this little man that I am. His love shouts, it dances, it hugs, it kisses, it laughs, it lifts. He seems unashamed of me, though I am often ashamed of myself. What a God! What salvation! What great grace! What a tsunami of weighty glory awaits those who begin to set their worshipful gaze upon Him!

Do you, like me, want to anchor your soul to such a kind Father, a wise Shepherd, a patient Teacher and a strong Counsellor?

But not simply to have Him **near** you, but have His strength *WITHIN* you and *UPON* you? To not only read His thoughts in scripture, (though that is divine!) but to hear His heart beat, catch His whispers, feel His breath. To have Him crown you with glory and honour, and turn your weakness into strength, your foolishness to wisdom, your poverty to riches!

Well here is what He is teaching me about how to fill my life with His strength every day, resulting in resilience, long suffering, stability and "Head on a pillow" peace in every circumstance:

"What You Focus On Grows"
It is a simple fact of life, and we have already discussed it, but remember that what you focus on will grow. Focus on skills and they'll develop. Focus on failure, you'll end up getting more of it! Ride a bicycle looking backwards, you'll crash.

Look intently at God in His presence and His word… can you guess what happens? … Calm, beautiful, awe inspired, mouth wide-open, heart-overwhelming peace, will flood our souls. Our minds will exchange fear for faith. Our emotions will give up stress and embrace rest. Our will softens. Our resolve deepens. Our worship stirs from deep inner recesses of spiritual potency, unlocked like the opening of flood gates. We feel truly, divinely, at peace and loved.

Don't Be Distracted

*"As Jesus and His disciples were on their way, He came to a village where a woman named Martha opened her home to Him. She had a sister called Mary, who sat at the Lord's feet listening to what He said. But **Martha was distracted** by all the preparations that had to be made. She came to Him and asked, "Lord, don't you care that my sister has left me to do the work by myself? Tell her to help me!" "Martha, Martha," the Lord answered, "you are worried and upset about many things, but only one thing is needed. **Mary has chosen what is better**, and it will not be taken away from her."* Luke 10:38-42

This is a beautifully illustrative picture of both focus and distraction. It teaches us about life with Jesus. Martha was distracted by legitimate duties; genuine needs and tasks that needed doing. "You're distracted, you're worried and upset about many things," Jesus said. But Mary had chosen better, and Martha was choosing poorly – Mary found purpose and peace, Martha found irritation, weakness, stress and upset.

There was something wonderfully abandoned about Mary. She had CHOSEN gazing, listening, hanging out with Jesus, above the practical niceties of a dinner party! (I have chosen poorly a million times in my life! How about you?)

If you are to discover the kind of strength God wants you to know, you're going to have to realise that many of the things you think you've got to do, or ought to do, or should do, are actually just things you WANT to do, but don't have to! There are some things that are eternally more important; like looking at Jesus.

Perfect Peace

Isaiah 26:3 says, *"You will keep in perfect peace him whose thoughts are fixed on you, because he trusts in you."*

That phrase "perfect peace." Oh I want that! It's "head on a pillow" peace in every storm. It means "completeness, safety, soundness (in body), welfare, health, prosperity, quiet, tranquility, contentment, friendship with God, especially in covenant relationship."

It says that this peace will come to those whose thoughts are fixed on Him. That means the one who fixes his frame of mind on God, will know perfect peace and wholeness. If I lean my mind on God, and not simply human experience or logical advice, if I am not distracted by the endless hankerings of this world, I will know divine peace. If, instead of being double minded, I can fix the eyes of my heart into a lasting "heart-gaze" on Him throughout my days, I will know the calm of His presence. Perfect peace.

Philippians 4:4-9 puts it this way: *"Rejoice in the Lord always. I will say it again: Rejoice! ... Do not be anxious about anything, but in everything, by prayer and petition, with thanksgiving, present your requests to God. And the peace of God, which transcends all understanding, will guard your hearts and your minds in Christ Jesus. Finally, brothers, **whatever is true, whatever is noble, whatever is right, whatever is pure, whatever is lovely, whatever is admirable--if anything is excellent or praiseworthy--think about such things.** ... And the God of peace will be with you."*

Something happens as we build focus into our lives, through the word of God, through casting our cares on Him, through worship and thankfulness, through meditating on His loveliness, through listening to His voice. As we gaze on Him His strength and goodness floods our lives!

In Luke's Gospel, Jesus talks about being "clothed with power from on high" (24:49) as the disciples "waited" on Him. There is a sense in which power, strength, ability and authority flows from heaven into our lives as we look to, expect, linger and wait on God.

Pick Up Your Lamp!

Luke 11:33-36 says *"No one lights a lamp and puts it in a place where it will be hidden, or under a bowl. Instead they put it on its stand, so that those who come in may see the light.* **Your eye is the lamp of your body. When your eyes are healthy, your whole body also is full of light.** *But when they are unhealthy, your body also is full of darkness. See to it, then, that the light within you is not darkness. Therefore, if your whole body is full of light, and no part of it dark, it will be just as full of light as when a lamp shines its light on you."*

Here Jesus teaches us that our eyes are like lamps, shining *INTO* our souls and bodies. What we gaze upon, will fill us. What we focus on, grows.

If our eyes are down in the darkness of despair, diagnosis, fears and worries, then depression and anxiety will flood our lives with darkness. But if we can get our "lamps" up into the light of God's presence, then glory, strength, power and hope will flood our whole beings.

How often do you get the eyes of your heart utterly focused on God?

How long can you hold His gaze?

How much time do you give to letting Him flood you with light, hope and peace?

How much are you leaning the framework of your mind on Him?

How often do you bask in His presence, asking Him to fill you with the power of His Holy Spirit?

Or like many, do you attend church on a Sunday (which is good!) but think like a pagan all week?! Are we Christians on Sundays and humanists all week? Do we worship with the saints on Sundays, but still worry with the world on Wednesdays? Are we all love on a Sunday and all logic on a Monday?

90 minutes of putting your "lamp on the lamp stand" of His presence each weekend will not make you strong. There must be daily habits, weekly devotions, monthly events and annual sabbaticals where you take time to re-focus, gaze on God, and be filled with the wonderful peace of heaven.

You see, life with Jesus is more than a self-improvement program. Your destiny is not simply based on what you have the skills or the money to achieve. No, we are allowed to live within His means, not ours. We can walk in His power, not just ours. We can embrace His will for our lives, and engage in divine exploits as we live filled with Him!

But only if we learn to focus, steadfastly, on Him.

Face The Rising Sun

"Because of the LORD's great love we are not consumed, for his compassions never fail. They are new every morning; great is your faithfulness." Lamentations 3:22-23

Most churches, cathedrals and temples are built facing east. They face Jerusalem, the Holy Land. They face the rising sun.

We too, are temples that must be built to face the rising sun of

God's daily new mercies. We need the frameworks of our mind to face the light of His presence in worship. To lift the eyes of our hearts to be flooded with the kindness, the hope and the glory of God.

Let His Goodness Pass Before You!

When Moses asked to see God's glory, God said "I will make my goodness pass before you." (Exodus 33:19). The glory of God is seen in the goodness of God. If you want to be filled with power, strength, authority and "head on a pillow" peace, gaze on Him. Take all the distractions of lower human life, place them to one side, and instead, teach your heart to focus on Jesus throughout the day. Retrain that worrier to be a worshipper. Replace logic with longing for Him. Don't just be human, be heavenly! Teach your soul to hold God's gaze. The longer you can hold His gaze, the more of His glory you'll experience.

Moses met God face to face (See Exodus 33:7+), but the moment he walked away from God, the glory started to lessen. The New International Version of the Bible calls it "fading glory." As he walked away from God, the reflecting glory dimmed. If he could have held God's gaze, he would have lived "from glory to glory." But he could not hold God's gaze permanently, as Moses was restricted by the fact that God would only encounter Moses in one geographical place, the tent of meeting.

But read what it says when discussing this very topic in 2 Corinthians chapters 3 and 4:

"For God, who said, "Let light shine out of darkness," made his light shine in our hearts to give us the light of the knowledge of God's glory displayed in the face of Christ." 2 Corinthian 4:6

In other words, God's glory is no longer waiting in a tent for us. Or even in a church service. It is not something we go to visit. But rather, we can be face to face with God in our hearts ALL DAY LONG, because God has made His glory shine in our hearts!

While we go about our day we can hold God's gaze. As we drive, we can worship face to face (Just don't close your eyes!) As we write, answer the phone, do the housework, the school run, or enjoy leisure, we can hold the gaze of God and meditate on His goodness, flooding our whole beings with light and peace.

The result of our focused temple, facing the daily rising sun of His goodness, will be strength, power and hope.

Which way is your temple facing? What is the prevailing attitude of your mind? A worrying mind will weaken you. A logical mind will distract you from the miraculous. A burdened mind will sap you of energy. An offended mind will cripple you with bitterness.

But as we enjoy God in our hearts, "always seeing what the Father is doing" as Jesus lived (John 5:19), our heads can rest on pillows of peace through every storm.

As we put aside distractions like Mary, we can sit at Jesus' feet, choosing what will bring us strength – moment by moment encounters through listening to Jesus.

As we lean the framework of our minds on Him, steadfastly fixing our inner gaze on His might, we will "rise up like eagles, run and not grow weary, walk and not faint" (Isaiah 40:31). Perfect peace will be ours.

As we rejoice in Him always, casting cares on Him and focusing intently and purposefully on what is lovely and admirable in life and in the Lord, then the God of peace will be with us.

As we build our temples facing the rising sun, we will discover "His mercies are new every morning," and the energy-sapping dullness of regret will be banished.

He is your Strength, your Peace, your Wisdom. "Everything He has is yours" (Luke 15:31). His grace is enough for you. He is a Refuge, a Strong Tower, a Fortress, a Rock. He is your Counsellor, your Wisdom, your Strategist, your Purpose.

He Is Your Strength

Look up. Look to Him. Worship. Gaze. Enjoy Him in your heart, and He will clothe you with strength!

"Look to the LORD and His strength; seek His face always."

Psalm 105:4

For Group Discussion:

1. What you focus on grows. This is true in negative and positive ways. Discuss.

2. How can we "gaze on God" more? How can we stop our hearts from being so distracted by small things, and more focused on God?

3. Has anyone in the group ever experience "Head on a pillow peace" in a crisis? Describe what happened.

4. Spend some time worshipping and asking God to fill you with the power of His Holy Spirit.

STRONGER

THE 40 DAY DEVOTIONAL

By Jarrod & Victoria Cooper
With Marion Cooper

THE 7 SECRETS OF STRENGTH
Jarrod Cooper

"Have I not commanded you? Be strong and courageous. Do not be afraid; do not be discouraged, for the Lord your God will be with you wherever you go." Joshua 1:9

The instruction to "Be strong" seems of huge importance, and yet so many Christians seem determined to make weakness fashionable. We are experts at it! The command to BE STRONG almost intimidates some of us.

But even in our obvious human weakness there must be a determination to find God's good strength to lift us to better days. Here are 7 ways to stay strong:

1. Keep Smiling. Nehemiah 8:10 *"Do not grieve, for the joy of the Lord is your strength"* is as true as ever. I find it so easy to get miserable, intense, disappointed, impatient and weak. But really you should enjoy the moment you are in. Be present. Suck the juice out of life and SMILE. If you get like me and wonder who the miserable old git in the mirror is, purposefully slap a smile on that face. It's an act of immense faith. And it's so good for your health.

2. Stay In Grace. So many genuinely, lovely Christians spend way too much time feeling guilty, shameful, wishing they were so much more. But *"there is a river whose streams make glad the city of God,"* a river of grace for you and me. Psalms 30:7 states *"When you favoured me, my mountain stood firm."* LET HIM favour you; it'll make you strong. Stop feeling like you wear God's grace out. Have a conscience, but don't be exhausted by an oversensitive one

that will not forgive you for things done or left undone, even after repentance. Stay in the place where grace is exalted. Let mercy triumph over judgement.

3. Be Confident! Isaiah 30:15 says *"in quietness & confidence (trust) is your strength."* Sometimes we need to not give in to the feeling of insecurity. We need to instruct our soul "be confident in God." Stand a little taller. Smile a little broader. Whisper some good Bible promises to ourselves in our low moments, to posture our lives with godly confidence. God likes it (Heb 11:6).

4. Get Your God Moments. *"Those who wait upon the Lord shall exchange strengths with Him"* states Isaiah 40:29. Even Jesus needed His God-moments, disappearing up mountains to find intimate, prayerful, minutes of divine exchange. Where and when are your moments? Plan them. Guard them. God isn't disappointed in you when you miss prayer - He is disappointed FOR you. You've missed a moment that will cause you to be strong, today. And don't compete with others in prayer - Just find what works for you and stick to it!

5. Be Filled With Power. Ephesians 6:10 *"Be strong in the power of His might."* God loves to clothe us in divine energy, authority and ability. Without His divine presence in our lives, we really have nothing to give. To a generation of church goers to whom Pentecost is sometimes a distant memory, I would emplore you to become hungry again to be awash with His glory, as was the early church. The result? A small handful of weakling disciples who turned the world upside down!

6. Be Authentic. God loves you, made you, designed you before the world began. And His power rests most fully on you being you - never you impersonating anyone else. So discover the divine blueprint God has for you and start to be comfortable in the skin

you're in. It brings such strength. Psalm 139 shows us all your days were written before any of them came to be. That means God was an author before He was a Creator. His favourite subject? YOU! Meditate on the joy of being you - and be thankful.

7. Be Weak To Be Strong. 2 Corinthians 12:9-10 makes it clear that our pathway to strength is in weakness. The authentic vulnerability of honesty regarding our weakness, draws God into our lives. Humility is a magnet to grace ("He gives grace to the humble" James 4:6), but pride is a rejection of His help. We must never revel or rejoice about our sinfulness, but laugh about our vulnerable inabilities. Then it gives God such glory when we succeed!

Prayer: *Heavenly Father, thank You that YOU make ME strong and even when I don't feel like it. I choose to keep smiling because the JOY of the Lord is MY Strength. I thank You for Your grace which covers me, Your power that fills me and Your protection that surrounds me. I choose to put my trust and confidence in You, trusting that as I wait in Your presence You will renew my strength.*

BE STRONG

Marion Cooper

"Finally, be strong in the Lord and in his mighty power."
Ephesians 6:10

What does it mean to "Be Strong?" It is not to be arrogant, bossy, loud or over opinionated.

It is a command, "Be Strong."

That's a bit scary, because the truth is, even the most mature of us don't always feel strong, but that is what I love about God. He gives us a command and then He gives us His Spirit to help us to fulfil it.

"My grace is sufficient for you, for My strength is made perfect in weakness." 2 Corinthians 12.9

Whilst praying for people during a ministry time at one of our church conferences, I came across a beautiful woman in obvious pain and distress, not physically, but emotionally and spiritually. Although I was not meant to be counselling at all, this woman began to tearfully speak of her pain, rejection, depression and fears. As I continued to pray, I felt a huge compassion for this woman who knew the sacrifice of Jesus, who was saved, and yet she was still bound. She was not free.

Then this compassion was quickly turned to anger at the enemy who can so lie and deceive us, and rob us of our freedom, our joy, our peace and our life. Why do we let him do it to us? Why do we lay down under his lies? How can he hoodwink us so easily? How can he make us, God's children, so weak and unhappy?

'Be aware of the devil's schemes,' the Bible says in 2 Corinthians 2:11. Be wary of any pity-party blame focussed counselling. Be cautious of a mind-set that says, *"poor me, how badly I have been treated."*

I, as much as anyone, and perhaps more than some, struggle with self-pity. But I have learned that to sit and dwell on my pain, hurt and rejection is unproductive and negative and turns me into what I do not want to be, a weak woman whom satan has bound. James 4:7 says, *"Submit to God, resist the devil and he will flee from you."*

1. "Submit to God" by declaring His creative word over your life. 'I am accepted.' 'I am forgiven'. 'I am chosen.' 'I am strong.' Speak it out loud so the enemy can hear!

2. "Submit to God" by seeking to bring your life into line with God's word, repent if the Holy Spirit convicts of any sin, e.g. unforgiveness.

3. "Resist the devil!" How is it that we know exactly how to get cross with our spouse and certainly know how to raise our voice with our children, but when it comes to resisting the devil, our assertiveness flies out of the window? The Bible says, *'Resist the devil and he has to flee from you.'* Command him to go, declare he has no part in your life. Let's be American and 'Kick his butt!' - Or let's be scriptural and 'Trample him under our feet!' Don't be polite and English; you're allowed to get angry, determined and aggressive!

4. Then fill your life and heart with positive food from God and His word. Speak to your soul as King David did, *"Why are you cast down O my soul, hope in God."* Psalm 42:5

Count your blessings.

A quote from my husband, *'What you feed grows, what you starve dies.'*

Feed your heart self pity, and it will grow.

Feed your heart on the affirmation of God's word and that will grow.

Starve your heart of negative thoughts, and they will die.

On a very practical level, look after yourself. Eat healthily, get enough sleep, take care of your appearance. See also if there is a trigger to depression or anxiety, and avoid it. I personally know, I have to get out of the house for a period each day, I hate being in the house all the time.

God has plans for you and me, plans to prosper us, to give us a hope and a future.

We mustn't allow the enemy to rob us of all God has for us.

Let us be strong and not easily captured.

Prayer: *Father God, thank You that You have not given me a spirit of fear (or depression, anxiety or weakness) but of love, power and a sound mind (2 Tim 1:7). Lord, You command me to be strong, so please take my weakness and exchange it for Your strength. I choose to feed my heart with Your word and starve my heart and mind of negative thoughts. I thank You that I am loved, I am accepted, I am forgiven and because of You, I AM STRONG!*

DAY 3
YOUR DAY OF BOLDNESS
Jarrod Cooper

"Be bold and very courageous." Joshua 1:7

"Be bold!" God told Joshua, four times, before he led Israel into their Promised Land.

All destiny requires a bold step at some point, and your future is no exception.

My problem is that I'm not naturally bold. I'm sure Reinhard Bonnke finds all this stuff easy. He probably glows in the dark, hears God audibly and is awoken by angels singing his name (I'm joking by the way).

But not me, I'm normal. I get irritable, fearful, wonder whether I'm getting it right. I'm ordinary, even slightly dysfunctional at times!

Anyone else a little broken like me?

The good news is, Reinhard doesn't shine in the dark. All Christians are rehabilitating sinners. We've all got weaknesses, fears and doubts. Most get that feeling regularly, like everyone else in the room "gets it," except you.

So, when God says He chooses the foolish, He was telling the truth. He empowers the ordinary, gives boldness to the broken. He gives dignity to the dysfunctional and LOVES the sinner.

But still, even in your brokenness, your destiny will have times when you have to be bold.

Maybe (as my family once experienced), it's the boldness of leaving everything - job, country, home and church - to obey God. Overcoming homelessness and without any human surety, my family stepped out, to step in to a promised "mission land" destiny in God abroad.

Maybe it's stepping out to trust God to buy something for God's work that you can't afford. Maybe it's a job or career change, a church move, a mission opportunity, a new ministry area or even the high price of a well-deserved holiday to rest. All may require boldness.

But how do you know if it is God telling you to step out in boldness, and not just too much pizza the night before? Here's a few hints:

First, let me note, the most common WRONG drive behind a bold move would be things like a mid-life "boredom crisis!" (I have endless of these!) But they are usually my insecurities at work, not God's wisdom. Anything driven by boredom, pride, ego, (the source of most pain & sin!) envy and comparison to what others are doing or have, is going to get you in trouble and make you rush ahead of God. Always put that stuff at the feet of Jesus, and find a restful place. You need to hear God, not your inner self whining.

Use an inner crisis that asks, *"am I doing enough with my life?"* as a launch pad to go and hear God - don't make mad, bold, inappropriate moves.

Here are the tests to see if it is God:
1. PEACE - James 3:17 shows us God's wisdom is full of peace. Do you genuinely feel deeply at peace, that God is speaking to

you. Get a note pad and pen and write down what you actually think God is saying. *(Be careful to read what He actually says, not a desired interpretation of it. E.g. "You shall go out with joy" may not mean that you are to date a girl called Joy!)*

2. PRESENCE - Sometimes we become doubtful, even if it's God. But while we may worry and fret when we look at the facts, the risks and the possible errors, think more about what God says when you're in His presence in prayer and worship. Wisdom is found in worship.

3. WORD - Remember God is never going to go against His word. So He's not telling you to steal a car, or never go to Church. He won't go against His own nature. So measure the issue at hand against the Bible.

4. COUNSEL OF MANY - *"Victory is assured with the counsel of many" Proverbs 15:22.* But only tell the right people. Mature people. People who have gone through a few "bold step" seasons themselves. Don't tell jealous brothers, but do talk to experienced fathers.

5. TIMING - Knowing the "what" of God's will is quite easy. Knowing the "when" is another matter. Most people are trying to run way ahead of God. So relax and just listen. When it's right, it will come to fruition.

Your day of boldness will come, whether it's this year, or another. So prepare for it in word, worship and relationships. You're going to need all the help you can get!

Action Point: *Get a note pad and a pen and write down what you feel God is saying to you right now.*

DAY 4
GREATNESS IS ON THE INSIDE OF YOU
Victoria Cooper

"...and [so that you will begin to know] what the immeasurable and unlimited and surpassing greatness of His [active, spiritual] power is in us who believe. These are in accordance with the working of His mighty strength which He produced in Christ when He raised Him from the dead and seated Him at His own right hand in the heavenly places." Eph1:19-20 AMP

Ever been asked.... *"If you could have a superpower, what would it be?"*

As a child I loved pretending I had superpowers and I would play with my best friend using my coat as a cape pretending I could fly or turn invisible.

Sometimes, as we grow up, we can be so aware of our humanity and fragility that we lose confidence, get realistic and become boring.

As Spirit-filled Christians we can easily undervalue and dismiss the glorious gift given to us in Christ Jesus. Christ died for so much more than our sins. He died so that we can be heirs with Him.

"And if [we are His] children, [then we are His] heirs also: heirs of God and fellow heirs with Christ [sharing His spiritual blessing and inheritance]." Romans 8:17AMP

These scriptures can easily be glossed over and not truly believed by many Christians.

It is part of our inheritance as God's children to step into all that Jesus died for, otherwise it's like being given a diamond necklace or a priceless watch and never wearing it.

I inherited some beautiful cut wine glasses from my grandmother after she passed away. I have no idea what they're worth but she never used them because they were too expensive. When I got married I bought a glass cabinet to showcase this cut glass just as she had done.

One day my husband decided to use them for a special occasion. I was so nervous they would get broken in some way. Fast forward 15 years and we still use these beautiful glasses today and sometimes it's not even a special occasion. Sometimes you have to push through fears to enjoy all you have been given!

God did something incredible for us by sacrificing His only Son. How can we choose not to access this incredible treasure when it cost Jesus His life?

"But we have this treasure in jars of clay to show that this all-surpassing power is from God and not from us." 2 Corinthians 4:7 NIV

Greatness is on the inside of you. Stop denying its power. It's not about your weakness or lack, it's about His greatness, His sacrifice, His incredible love for us.

"By his divine power, God has given us everything we need for living a godly life. We have received all of this by coming to know him, the one who called us to himself by means of his marvelous glory and excellence. And because of his glory and excellence, he has given us great and precious promises. These are the promises that enable you to share his divine nature." 2 Peter1:3-4 NLT

His divine power runs through my veins. In the greek it's called "Zoe" life: God's eternal life flowing through me and through you!

Don't disqualify yourself from accessing all Christ died for. You are not here to endure life, you are here to live life abundantly in all of its fullness.

Jesus said,
"I tell you, whoever believes in me will do the works I have been doing, and they will do even greater things than these, because I am going to the Father." John 14:12 NIV

He has empowered you, He has qualified you, He approves of you and He has chosen to use you. Choose now to step into *"the immeasurable and unlimited and surpassing greatness of His [active, spiritual] power (which) is in us who believe."*

Prayer: *Jesus, thank You that because of Your death I can have life, Zoe life! The same power that raised You from the dead now lives in me. Your divine power has given me all that I need to live a godly life. Jesus, emanate through me. Help me to be Your hands and feet so that people will experience Your power through me. When I lay hands on the sick, they will be healed because You are in me and I am in You.*

HOW TO THRIVE IN LIFE
Jarrod Cooper

"The righteous will THRIVE like a palm tree, planted in the house of the Lord." Psalm 92:12

To thrive means to grow, develop, to prosper, to flourish or blossom ... and that's exactly what God wants for your life!

The Bible gives us two ways we can thrive:

Be Active
Jewish philosopher Martin Buber recalls: *"My grandfather was lame. Once they asked him to tell a story about his teacher, and he related how his master used to hop and dance while he prayed. My grandfather rose as he spoke and was so swept away by his story that he himself began to hop and dance to show how the master had done. From that hour he was cured of his lameness."*

Sharing and involvement does something inside us. It heals us, strengthens us, changes our hearts.
Ephesians 4:16 tells us that the church (you!) will grow mature *"as each part does it's work."* You have unique gifts, talents and strengths – and if we are going to grow stronger, we need to be active.

If you want your church to feel like your true spiritual home, a place to grow and blossom, join a team, clean a floor, put some work in - it will change your heart as you do! Without it you are just a consumer, not a relative.

Be Connected

The other way to thrive is to be connected.

There's a Spanish story of a father and son who had become estranged. The son ran away, and the father set off to find him. He searched for months to no avail. Finally, in a last desperate effort to find him, the father put an advert in a Madrid newspaper. The ad read: *"Dear Paco, meet me in front of this newspaper office at noon on Saturday. All is forgiven. I love you. Your Father."* On the Saturday, 800 *"Pacos"* showed up, looking for forgiveness and love from their fathers.

We live in a society that, like our 800 Pacos, is more lonely and disconnected than ever. Have you noticed that in a church service you might be close to people physically, but miles apart emotionally?

Psalm 92:12 says, *"The righteous will THRIVE like a palm tree, planted in the house of the Lord."* To be planted you need to allow your roots to go down deep into real friendships. Do you have real, close friends in your church family? If not, then now is the time to dig in deeper.

Do this by joining a small group or being in a small team. I love meeting with my group of around 16 friends, to eat, laugh, talk, plan and pray together. It's not enough for me to be in large meetings – I have to let myself be rooted in friendships.

Life is better lived in circles than rows. Crowds who sit in rows in auditoriums must become circles of friends around meal tables. It's how we are designed to be rooted.

I heard someone say, *"People don't want to go to a friendly church - they want friends."* In other words, it's about real friendships, not just bigger smiles from Stewards or organised pastoral care teams. We need to take time to build some friendships, and we will thrive!

Doing and connecting - both will help you thrive in life.

Prayer: *Heavenly Father, thank You for Your word. It brings life to my mortal bones. Thank You for the body of Christ. We all have a part to play and I pray You will help me to be all You want me to be in _____ (enter name of your church). Help me to be a blessing to others and pleasing in Your sight. Give me God-given friendships that I can bless and that will also be a blessing to me. I want to thrive in Your house Oh Lord.*

DAY 6
LIVE BY FAITH, NOT BY SIGHT
Victoria Cooper

"For we walk by faith, not by sight [living our lives in a manner consistent with our confident belief in God's promises]." 2 Corinthians 5:7 AMP

So often we can forget that we are to "walk by faith" as Christians. Our senses can be so heightened by all that's going on around us - Work, family, friends, social media, bills and health.

Whether life is going well or feels difficult, we can feel like we are being tossed to and fro by the winds of change, opinions, problems, feelings and moods. James 1 says,

"The one who doubts is like a wave of the sea, blown and tossed by the wind." James 1:6 NIV

Have you ever come back from a holiday with "post holiday blues syndrome" or from an awesome mission and you come from a huge high to a disgruntled low?

While this may be a very common thing, we cannot let our feelings or emotions dictate our lives.

Smith Wigglesworth once said,
"I am not moved by what I feel. I am not moved by what I see. I am moved only by what I believe."

This is more easily said than done when your bank balance is low and bills are waiting to be paid or the doctor's diagnosis comes back with your worst fear.

We are told in Hebrews 4:12 that the word of God is powerful.

"For the word of God is living and active and full of power [making it operative, energizing, and effective]. It is sharper than any two-edged sword, penetrating as far as the division of the soul and spirit [the completeness of a person], and of both joints and marrow [the deepest parts of our nature], exposing and judging the very thoughts and intentions of the heart." Hebrews 4:12 AMP

We read in the Gospels that when Jesus spoke to the storm, it calmed down at His word. When He spoke to sickness, it disappeared.

God's word in our mouth is powerful! This is why we should speak out scripture and believe it will impact our lives and the situations we are going through.

I have come up against difficulties in my own life and at times, my mind has gone completely blank when it comes to confessing scripture. My emotions have often filled my mind instead of the word of God.

This is not how we are meant to live. We are not to live by our feelings or by what we see, but by what the word of God says...

You feel worried? The word of God for you says...

"Do not be anxious about anything, but in every situation, by prayer and petition, with thanksgiving, present your requests to God. And the peace of God, which transcends all understanding, will guard your hearts and your minds in Christ Jesus." Philippians 4:6-7 NIV
You feel depressed? The word of God for you says...

"The Spirit of the Sovereign Lord is on me, because the Lord has anointed me to proclaim good news to the poor. He has sent me to bind up the brokenhearted, to proclaim freedom for the captives and release from darkness for the prisoners, and provide for those who grieve in Zion— to bestow on them a crown of beauty instead of ashes, the oil of joy instead of mourning, and a garment of praise instead of a spirit of despair. They will be called oaks of righteousness, a planting of the Lord for the display of his splendour." Isaiah 61:1, 3 NIV

Are you in financial trouble? The word of God for you says…

"Give, and it will be given to you. They will pour into your lap a good measure--pressed down, shaken together, and running over [with no space left for more]. For with the standard of measurement you use [when you do good to others], it will be measured to you in return." Luke 6:38 AMP

Are you sick? The word of God for you says…

"He himself bore our sins" in his body on the cross, so that we might die to sins and live for righteousness; "by his wounds you have been healed." 1 Peter 2:24 NIV

Do you feel ugly? The word of God for you says….
"For you created my inmost being; you knit me together in my mother's womb. I praise you because I am fearfully and wonderfully made; your works are wonderful, I know that full well. My frame was not hidden from you when I was made in the secret place, when I was woven together in the depths of the earth. Your eyes saw my unformed body; all the days ordained for me were written in your book before one of them came to be." Psalm 139:13-16 NIV

The Bible is full of verses to direct and help our faith. At times we may not feel or see God's perspective, but we cannot rely on emotions or natural eyesight. We must believe it, because faith is the currency of heaven - asking and trusting is the only way we can release heaven's resources into our lives.

This is how God works.

Action Point: *Why don't you read through these scriptures again? Believe them, confess them and declare them over your life.*

A STRATEGY FOR LIFE
Marion Cooper

"Every part of scripture is God breathed and useful one way or another- showing us truth, exposing our rebellion, correcting our mistakes, training us to live God's way. Through the word, we are put together and shaped up for the tasks God has for us." 2 Tim 3.16 (The Message)

When I first became a Christian, over 58 years ago, I was given a little booklet emphasising the importance of 2 Timothy 2:15. *"Be diligent to present yourself approved to God, a worker who does not need to be ashamed, rightly dividing the word of truth." (NKJV)*

I don't know if I totally understood its meaning then or if I fully do today. But the message it placed in my heart has remained with me all these years and is the theme of almost all my ministry and certainly my life values: The Bible holds the secret for a strategy for life and if we seek to live by it, by His help, we will live successful lives, well pleasing to Him.

In the years that followed my conversion, and certainly while we have been in church leadership, I have been deeply distressed by the number of Christians leading damaged and defeated lives in at least certain areas. During ministry, counselling or just generally talking, it has become clear that what many are seeking isn't necessarily a modern phenomena, because it was also the request of Naaman to Elisha, *"Call upon your God, wave your hand over me and heal my leprosy." 2 Kings 5:11*

I certainly understand that desire, I too would like instantaneous answers to my problems!

"Lord wave your magic wand and change my spouse, my child, my bank account, my health, my addictions, my bad habits, change my life, now!" Sometimes by His grace, God does just that, but much more often, my experience has been that God is there to help, direct, guide and encourage. His plan is that we have "a strategy for life" and work out our own problems, until we come to a place of victory in that area.

The book of Proverbs sings the virtues of wisdom for life. "Do this" and you will succeed, "do that" and you will fail. James 1:5 tells us that if we lack wisdom, we should ask God for it and He, without recriminations, will give it to us. Wisdom in our finances, wisdom in our marriages, wisdom to raise our children, wisdom in our ministries, wisdom in our jobs, wisdom in our relationships, wisdom to stay fit and well. Let me give you an example.

If I was deeply in debt, I am pretty certain that my desire would be that God would come and turn my "red" bank balance to "black" immediately! I would certainly be praying and seeking God about this need. But Godly wisdom says I should look at why I am in debt. Am I unwise in my spending, do I have a budget? Where could I economise? Am I honouring God and tithing? Have I caught this world's materialism and credit culture?

A more mature prayer would be, *"God help me to get out of this mess and give me wisdom with my finances."* If God did come and immediately wipe out our debts, there is a really strong probability that without altering our behaviour, we would soon be back in exactly the same position as before.

God gives us wisdom so that we can retrain ourselves in that area, so we become overcoming and victorious and not defeated. He gives us that strategy for life, the vast majority of which can be found in His Word.

Let me just counter this by saying, when we know there is absolutely nothing more we can do, that we are living wise, obedient lives, that's when He will come in and miraculously change the situation.

In our years in Gibraltar, living as missionaries on a very meagre pay and raising two children, being extremely economical with our money, we at times knew totally miraculous financial provision. During one period, each month a bundle of bank notes was pushed into our post box, no envelope, no note, nothing - just miraculous provision.

When we become Christians, we are told to "walk in the Spirit," but that doesn't require that we remove our brains! God's plan for us is that we become mature and perfect, lacking nothing. God's plan for us, His people, is that we have life skills, that we have wisdom, that in our every day ordinary lives, we glorify Him. God's plan for us, is that by His wisdom, we are role models to the world, and that they seek our advice.

When I look into God's word, I want to know how can I live a victorious, joyful, overcoming life for Jesus today. How can I avoid depression and unforgiveness? How can I raise my teenage son? How can I keep my marriage happy and passionate? How can I walk closer with Jesus? How can I be a testimony today?

Prayer: *Thank You Father for Your word. It is life to me. It is a lamp to my feet and a light to my path. It brings direction and instruction in to my life. Thank You for Your wisdom and right now I ask for wisdom in _____ (tell God what you currently need wisdom for and give time to listening to God for direction.)*

I CLING TO YOU

Victoria Cooper

"I cling to you; your strong right hand holds me securely." Psalm 63:8 NLT

It's never easy weathering a storm, especially one that threatens complete destruction like a hurricane.

It's been devastating to watch TV footage of the latest hurricanes ripping through beautiful Caribbean islands. Homes, trees and lives lost.

The marine life suffers too, as storm surges and huge waves destroy coral reefs and washes up fish and crabs. But there's one simple creature that impresses me when the storms roll in...The Limpet.

During storms they cling to the rocks they live on and it's near-impossible to dislodge them once they've clamped down. There's something we can mirror here from this humble sea creature.

Psalm 63 says, *"I cling to you; your strong right hand holds me securely."* Psalm 63:8 NLT

We all face or have faced storms in life that turn our world upside down, causing pain and fear and perhaps loss.

Whilst David was running for his life he cried out to God again and again in the Psalms...

"Truly he is my rock and my salvation; he is my fortress, I will not

be shaken." Psalm 62:6 NIV

David weathered storm after storm through his life but his faith was "clamped" on God his rock. He was not shaken.

Sometimes the meteorologists will predict a storm will get worse before it'll get better. Joseph knew this to be true:

For a young man with such promise and purpose his life took a turn for the worst. Bullied and sold as a slave by his own brothers (Gen 37), and then later thrown into prison left to die (Genesis 39), Joseph went from favoured to falsely accused. He couldn't have been further from his dreams!

In prison he had to dig deep into the well of his own spirit, press in and connect with God. God was all he had to cling to, and through this storm Joseph chose to "clampdown" on to God his rock, which eventually led to the fulfillment of his dreams.

"As for you, you meant evil against me, but God meant it for good." Genesis 50:20 AMP

Whatever storm you're going through, don't let it destroy you, or toss you around in its violent waves. Cling to the rock, clamp down and hold on to God. It may just be that this storm will be the making of you.

"I hold on to you for dear life, and you hold me steady as a post." Psalm 63:8 MSG

Action Point: *Put on some worship music and spend some time in God's presence. Let Him be your rock, your strong tower. His presence is a place to hide during the storms of life.*

DAY 9
ANCHOR LINES
Marion Cooper

"When your words came I ate them, they were my joy and my hearts delight." Jeremiah 15:16

If hearing from God is so important, especially in aiding us to persevere, what should we be doing with that word when God drops it into our lives?

What we cannot and must not do, is let those precious words float off into the atmosphere or they are useless. They only have power in our lives as we take hold of them, stand on them and assimilate them.

Some years ago, I went on holiday to the Greek island of Corfu and whilst there I took a boat trip around some of the smaller Greek islands. We eventually moored off the island of Antipaxos and the captain let down the anchor and said we could all swim ashore to a deserted white beach, only accessible from the sea. The brave youngsters leapt over the side of the boat into the turquoise waters. A few others carefully descended the ladder, gently slipping into the warm waters, and a few older ones or non swimmers remained on deck!

Now I am not a good swimmer, but looking into those stunning waters, I realised I may never have the opportunity again to swim in these azure seas. Carefully I climbed down the ladder and with my preferred stroke of 'doggy paddle' proceeded to the beach. Some 20 minutes later, the captain sounded the ships siren, the signal to get back on board, we were setting sail again. To a man, everyone launched themselves into the sea and began to swim energetically back to our boat.

I allowed the now churning sea to calm down, then carefully waded as far as I could before beginning my 'doggy paddle' return. It was only as I approached the boat that I realised there was a "people jam" as everyone now waited to climb up the only ladder! I slightly panicked until I saw the massive, strong white anchor rope already supporting a number of people.

With great relief I joined them, wrapping my arms securely around the rope, intending to wait until the ladder had cleared and I could climb aboard. All was well until the captain began to shout and order us off his anchor rope! Everyone obeyed and let go except me. Now you need to know, I am a law keeper and not a law breaker by nature, but not when my life is at risk. I totally ignored him, even avoiding looking in his direction.

People around me began to draw my attention to what he was saying, I in turn continued to ignore them all and cling to the anchor rope. I was not letting go of my security no matter what anyone said or did.

I clung onto that anchor line until the queue at the ladder had cleared and I could swim that small distance and climb safely on board.

That is exactly what we should do with God's words in our lives! Cling on to it with all our strength, no matter what anyone says or does.

Prayer: *Thank You Father God for Your word. It anchors my soul and keeps me safe. I meditate on Your word and let it dwell in my heart, permeating my mind and saturating my soul. Your word is powerful, it is life and light to me, bringing wisdom and direction.*

I WILL BE WHAT I WILL BE
Victoria Cooper

"God said to Moses, "I AM WHO I AM*" Exodus 3:14
(*I WILL BE WHAT I WILL BE)

God's desire is to partner with us. He wants to will and to act through us. (Phil 2:13)

Moses was minding his own business when God called Him to deliver the Israelites out of Egypt. If you're familiar with the story, you will know Moses' first reaction....

"Who am I that I should go to Pharaoh and bring the Israelites out of Egypt?" Exodus 3:11 NIV

"O Lord, I'm not very good with words. I never have been, and I'm not now, even though you have spoken to me. I get tongue-tied, and my words get tangled." Exodus 4:10 NLT

Can you relate? I certainly can. God's reaction was this....

"I will be with you." Exodus 3:12 NIV

Then He follows this in verse 14 by saying,

"I AM WHO I AM" or as some translations put it, "I WILL BE WHAT I WILL BE."

God has numerous names that describe who He is.....HEALER, PROVIDER, SHIELD, COMFORTER... but I want to focus on the I WILL BE WHAT I WILL BE.

Just take a look at these scriptures that tell us what God WILL BE to us, through us and in us:

"I will bless those who bless you." Genesis 12:3 NIV

"I will make you very fruitful." Genesis 17:6 NIV

"I will help you speak and will teach you what to say." Exodus 4:12 NIV

"My Presence will go with you, and I will give you rest." Exodus 33:14 NIV

"I will cause all my goodness to pass in front of you, and I will proclaim my name, the LORD, in your presence. I will have mercy on whom I will have mercy, and I will have compassion on whom I will have compassion." Exodus 33:19 NIV

"I will give you every place where you set your foot, as I promised Moses." Joshua 1:3 NIV

"I will be his father, and he will be my son. I will never take my love away from him." 1 Chronicles 17:13 NIV

"I will deliver you." 2 Kings 20:6 NIV

"I will instruct you and teach you in the way you should go; I will counsel you with my loving eye on you." Psalm 32:8 NIV

"I will rescue him; I will protect him, for he acknowledges my name. He will call on me, and I will answer him; I will be with him in trouble, I will deliver him and honour him. With long life I will satisfy him and show him my salvation." Psalm 91:14-16 NIV

"I will make rivers flow on barren heights, and springs within the valleys. I will turn the desert into pools of water, and the parched ground into springs." Isaiah 41:18 NIV

"I will put my Spirit on him."
"I will take hold of your hand. I will keep you."
"I will lead the blind by ways they have not known, along unfamiliar paths I will guide them; I will turn the darkness into light before them and make the rough places smooth." Isaiah 42:1,6,16 NIV

"I will go before you and will level the mountains; I will break down gates of bronze and cut through bars of iron. I will give you hidden treasures, riches stored in secret places."
"I will strengthen you." Isaiah 45:2-3, 5 NIV

"I will carry you; I will sustain you and I will rescue you." Isaiah 46:4 NIV

"I will refresh the weary and satisfy the faint." Jeremiah 31:25 NIV

"I will make an everlasting covenant with them: I will never stop doing good to them, and I will inspire them to fear me, so that they will never turn away from me. I will rejoice in doing them good and will assuredly plant them in this land with all my heart and soul." Jeremiah 32:40-41 NIV

"I will bring health and healing to it; I will heal my people and will let them enjoy abundant peace and security." Jeremiah 33:6 NIV

"I will make them and the places surrounding my hill a blessing. I will send down showers in season; there will be showers of

blessing." Ezekiel 34:26 NIV

"I will save you from all your uncleanness. I will call for the grain and make it plentiful and will not bring famine upon you. I will increase the fruit of the trees and the crops of the field, so that you will no longer suffer disgrace among the nations because of famine." Ezekiel 36:29-30 NIV

"I will make a covenant of peace with them; it will be an everlasting covenant. I will establish them and increase their numbers, and I will put my sanctuary among them forever. My dwelling place will be with them; I will be their God, and they will be my people." Ezekiel 37:26-27 NIV

"I will deliver this people from the power of the grave; I will redeem them from death." Hosea 13:14 NIV

"I will make you fishers of men." Matt 4:19 NKJ

"I will give you rest." Matthew 11:28 NIV

"I will go ahead of you." Matthew 26:32 NIV

WOW!!!

This is powerful. This is God's word to you.

No more excuses…He will make you fruitful, He will protect you, He will sustain you, He will guide you, He will heal you, He will help you, He will make you, He will go ahead of you.

Prayer: *Thank You Heavenly Father that You want to partner with me. As I submit to You, trust You, Lean and rely on You, You will prove Yourself to me. You will act on my behalf and make a way where there is no way. You are an awesome God, the great I AM.*

This covenant and this relationship means everything to me. I worship You, Almighty God!

DAY 11

HE WILL UPHOLD YOU

Jarrod Cooper

"Here is my servant, who I uphold." Isaiah 42:1

This verse shows a wonderful insight into God's care for Jesus, as He walked out His purpose on the earth. The Father was committed to "upholding the Son."

And as His servants today, He is committed to upholding you and me too.

You can relax in the incredible promise today, that He will lift you up, carry you, strengthen you and bring you through. He has made it His responsibility.

Verse 4 of Isaiah 42 promises that *"He will not falter nor be discouraged."*

God has even promised to stop you faltering; He'll lift you up, so your ankle will not turn. As Psalm 91 puts it, His angels will *"lift you up in their hands, so your foot will not strike the stones"* Psalm 91:11-12.

You won't even need to be discouraged if you stay close to God. Just turn to His word when discouragement looms, and His Spirit will stir afresh the confidence to keep going on.

Your success is His responsibility, more than yours!

I find the reassuring promise of God to "fulfil His purpose for me" helps me relax.

My call, my very life, was all His idea, and indeed in one very real sense, it is His responsibility to bring it about, not mine! I simply co-operate to the best of my ability, though even that ability truly comes from Him!

So how does God intervene, support and help us fulfil this divine destiny? You have to remember God isn't just a theoretical group of principles - God is a "doer."

Isaiah 42:16 says, *"I will turn the darkness into light before them and make the rough places smooth. These are the things I will do; I will not forsake them."*

Sometimes I forget that God is not just a comforter, a source of truth or a relief from fear or guilt - God is a DOER. "These are the things I WILL DO" He says in this wonderful promise.

Got problems? Situations that need to shift? Bills, relationships, sickness, threats, job losses or organisational difficulty? The Good News is - GOD IS A DOER! True, sometimes He does just "talk you through it" - but sometimes He actually does it all for you!

Lay your problems all before Him, pour it out, casting all your cares on Him, and you're going to find He'll care for you! He'll "Make rough places smooth. Turn darkness into light." Things actually change when we get God involved.

Money arrives in the post; sickness and pain leaves by the morning; threatening people leave; bad attitudes vanish; we get promoted instead of fired; electrical items get fixed! He does stuff!

Let Him make some incredible changes to your life, by calling Him into your situation. Let Him DO something wonderful!

Action Point: *In what areas of your life do you need God's intervention right now? List them, write them down or pray them out loud to Him daily - and trust God to do incredible things in your life.*

DAY 12
A DIVINE DIAGNOSIS
Jarrod Cooper

"Anyone who is in Christ, is a new creation" 2 Corinthians 5:17

Let's pretend, for one moment, that I am a divine doctor and that I can scan your spiritual being with medical devices. Let's also pretend that a man came to my office, having visited a church and prayed the "sinners prayer," and now he is beginning to wonder about the changes going on in him. Well, this is what I would say:

My dear man, I have some very good news for you. I have scanned your entire body, soul and spirit and found something. I have indeed seen what is causing these changes in your life. I have diagnosed you with a virulent, aggressive case of JESUS dwelling in your heart (Ephesians 3:17)!

This means you are going to go through some rapid changes, and there is very little I can do about it. JESUS can be quite fast acting, often simply overwhelming the normal functions of your being. When people catch JESUS there are some common symptoms that occur: Your body will begin to be protected and strengthened. Your anti-bodies will work better, your stress levels will decrease and you will fight off every disease, sickness and injury. Your body will repair quicker than normal and many diseases will simply bounce off you without you even knowing they came knocking.

This aggressive case of JESUS will make you more patient, loving, long-suffering and kind. Where as before you caught JESUS, your love would become depleted, now a deeper sense of security and approval will fill your life, leading to stronger feelings of grace and compassion toward others.

Being infected with JESUS means that many giftings are heightened, strengthened and begin to appear in your life. Sometimes it's like JESUS has a life of His own, and you will begin to think thoughts, have feelings and longings that seem far more noble, sacrificial and bold than you would think sensible. It is as though He is fully living in you, though you will never actually lose your free will entirely.

With such a severe case of JESUS I would expect you to be taken over until your whole soul and spirit feels as though it is in heaven itself. Wisdom, peace, love and strength tends to increase year by year and when you eventually die, you find that death has no sting anymore.

Now, it is entirely possible for this condition to go into remission and fade over time, but continual trust, reading of the Bible, prayer and a concentrated obsession with what you have caught will only strengthen it. The only way to get rid of this change is to completely ignore it as if nothing has happened.

I have to tell you though, you will never be the same again if you keep obsessing on what you have caught, as those who truly build their lives around the identity of their condition, tend to become entirely new creations, not even remotely resembling their original self. In short, life will forever be different, downright heavenly in fact!"

How's that for a diagnosis?!

Prayer: *Oh Jesus I want to be completely and utterly filled with You. I want my whole being to be consumed by You so that everyone knows and sees You in me. Holy Spirit fill me right now* *and if there is any area in me that has grown cold I pray you will light an ember deep in my soul and blow through me until I am on fire for You!*

DAY 13
I WENT IN RESPONSE
Jarrod Cooper

"I went in response to a revelation..." Galatians 2:2

What has God said to you lately? When is the last time you heard His voice? Do you sense a flow of the wisdom of heaven in your world today?

Paul says, *"He went in response to a revelation..."* Everything in our lives begins in the mind of God, and flows to us through the multi-media of heaven's communication. A thought, a feeling, a hunch, a Bible verse, seemingly coming to life and jumping off the page can often be God speaking.

Whenever this happens, I write it down. The verse, the feeling, the nudge, even the exact words, on the occasions it comes with such clarity. I do this because I know when God speaks, He has some blessing, some good thing in mind, for me or someone I love. A miracle is ready to unfold!

I remember walking into a car show-room, looking for a new car for my travelling ministry. The only problem was that I had no money. To my surprise, I saw a new car and God said, "book it!"

"I have no money" I complained to God - but there was no doubting that it was the same still small voice that tells me to do easier things - so I had to conclude I should book it!

Within days of me actually needing to pay for the car, I received a cheque for thousands of pounds, which covered the costs. Miracles are simply the result of acting in obedience to what you hear.

Another time a friend of mine was praying for someone with Fibromyalgia. She felt that God said "Lift your walking stick over your head." In pain, the suffering friend did, and she was completely healed, even handing back a no longer needed disability badge for her car!

Still another friend felt God say to put lemon juice on her own arthritic joints. After years of pain my friend awoke the next morning completely healed!

Now, booking brand new cars you can't afford, lifting sticks over your head and putting lemon juice on arthritic joints is not the normal way to go about life! But you're not normal! God's voice wants to lead you into miracles! When God speaks, waving a staff over the sea can part it (Exodus 14:16), shouting at walls will make them fall (Joshua 6:5) and washing in a river can heal you (2 Kings 5:10), IF and WHEN God says to do these things.

We must never make a repetitive culture out of what God says to do only once, because sticks don't part seas and shouts don't flatten castles like Jericho. The power is only in listening to the voice of God right here, right now. There are miracles in recognising those gold-embossed thoughts, that seem to come from some peaceful place, deep inside our hearts, where God whispers, "Do this, and I'll do that."

If you want to start enjoying heavens adventures for your life, then start listening. From there, start responding. When you do, life is going to get incredibly exciting!

Prayer: *Dear Jesus, thank You that I can hear Your voice. Teach me to recognise which thoughts are from You, whispering deep in my spirit. Let me go on the adventure of hearing Your voice, today!*

DAY 14
A TIME TO LOVE AND A TIME TO HATE
Jarrod Cooper

"There are six things The Lord hates, seven that are detestable to Him." Proverbs 6:16

Psalm 11:5 tells us that "God's soul hates the wicked." Ever thought about that? God has the capacity to hate; to find things, even people's behaviour, detestable.

In modern, western, society, especially in the Church, I think there is sometimes a pressure for us to lose the extremes of true love and hate, and replace it with a bland, politically correct, mind numbing politeness. We neither love nor hate; we tolerate, nod and remain silent. We avoid offering true and full opinions for fear of offence. We shuffle along hoping to avoid the extremes we were actually designed to express.

Yet God is far more extreme; and that's OK! He loves. He hates. He gushes, gets hot tempered. He gets jealous for us, passionate even. He dances, hugs, shouts, turns over tables, lets "zeal consume Him" (yes, I have scriptures for all of those). It's part of being fully alive.

Perhaps today is a day to be really like our God. Make today a day to truly LOVE. Decide that it's OK to openly honour a leader and show your support without feeling smarmy. It's OK to write a friend a card, or an encouragement on their social media page. We may even use the "L" word - (I "Love" you). Today is the day to be wide-eyed about creation. To shed a tear over a movie (C'mon guys!). To shout or dance a little in worship to God. To do something wildly generous to someone who doesn't deserve it. It's

134

a day to love.

I do believe it's healthier to spend more time loving than hating; and we must avoid the extremes of becoming self righteous or judgmental - but to be truly godly, we must also make it a day to HATE!

Let's hate slander, and sometimes even tell the slanderer to stop, without fear of their funny looks! Let's detest sexual sin, drunkenness, stealing or gossip, and tell others we don't approve, when we need to. Let's detest human trafficking; complain to the shop that places "adult" material in a child's view; firmly stand our ground in our desire for biblical morality.

There are times to let out the fact that we really, really don't like some things about society, and stop bottling, ignoring and shuffling by like the masses, all for the British sake of "not causing a fuss!" Some days, it's a day to hate like God hates.

It just might change the world in which we live.

Action Point: *Take some moments today to ask yourself if there are areas of your life where you are too passive. Are you failing to fully express love to those around you? Are you too accepting of people being manipulative of you, rude to you or even abusive of you? Being a Christian doesn't mean you necessarily have to tolerate that. Also, are you too accepting of your own sin? Passivity regarding what the Bible calls as sin, will also make you weak. Finally, is there something God has called you to do to change society that you are avoiding because of potential persecution? The world cannot be shaped unless we speak up!*

Pray and ask God for clarity, grace and truth - and the boldness to be all God has called you to be!

BE ALERT, GET INDIGNANT
Marion Cooper

'We are not ignorant of his (the devil's) schemes.' 2 Corinthians 2:11

We were driving on the motorway a while ago and found ourselves behind a lorry that repeatedly swerved on to the hard shoulder. It was obvious the driver was either tired or very distracted. (As we overtook him he was texting!)

It brought home to me afresh how dangerous it is to be unaware of our surroundings, not of course just in driving but in life's journey.

This incident, along with hearing that so many of our Christian friends across the world had come under serious attack, set off alarm bells.

The Bible tells us to be alert, on guard, watchful and vigilant. Why? Because we have an enemy. We Christians have an all powerful, all victorious and conquering God but we also have an adversary, an enemy. He comes, the Bible warns us, to blind our eyes, to steal God's word from our hearts, to accuse, murder, steal, kill and destroy, to tempt us and lay sickness on us.

1 Corinthians 2.14-15 talks of the man of the Spirit being 'discerning,' seeing clearly, having insight into what is actually happening in the spiritual realm around us.

2 Corintians 2:11 says, *"We are not ignorant of his (the devil's) schemes."*

Yet I believe we often are ignorant, unaware, not discerning of his activities.

One of the devil's ploys when we are under attack is to persuade us that this is life. It is hereditary, our age, our fault, part of the course and we are blind to the real cause, do nothing and accept it!

In the story of David and Goliath, King Saul and all his army did nothing about the daily threats from Goliath yet were *"dismayed and terrified."*

It took the young shepherd boy David to come into camp, hear these threats and get indignant!

"Who is this uncircumcised Philistine that he should defy the armies of the living God." (1 Samuel 17:26)

David knew who he was and, probably more importantly, whose he was. He also understood where this attack was coming from.

Just like David we need to get indignant for ourselves, and also for the church family. How dare the enemy lay sickness, cancer, poverty, discord, depression, stress and anxiety on us! How dare he seek to steal our children and our grandchildren away from Jesus!

As David actually faced up to the giant enemy, his words are a pattern for all of us who face "giants" in our lives.

"You come against me with sword, spear and javelin, but I come against you in the name of the Lord Almighty, the God of the armies of Israel whom you have defied.......The battle is the Lord's." 1 Samuel 17:45;47

We have an authority to deal with such attacks, not in our own strength but in Jesus.

In Ephesians 1, Paul prays that *"we may know His incomparably great power for us who believe...like the working of His mighty strength when He raised Christ from the dead...And seated Him far above all rule, authority, power and dominion."* (18-21)

As well as resisting Satan, chief among the weapons God has given us is worship and praise. They enthrone God to deal directly with the enemy giants in our lives. Our God is a warrior!

Be alert, get indignant, know who we are in Jesus and whose we are and the incomparably great power invested in us who believe.

"No in all these things we are more than conquerors through Him who loved us." Romans 8:37

Prayer: *Heavenly Father, I thank You that the devil is defeated! You made a complete exhibition of him when You died and rose to life. Exuberant victory is mine through Jesus Christ. I am more than a conqueror. I choose to put on the whole armour of God. I equip myself with truth, righteousness, faith & peace. I am strong in the Lord because Your word dwells within me.*

INSIDE EVERY ACORN IS AN OAK TREE

Victoria Cooper

*They will be called oaks of righteousness, a planting of the Lord
for the display of His splendour." Isaiah 61:3*

Inside every acorn is an entire forest. Every oak tree produces
immeasurable acorns so the potential of a simple acorn is limitless.

Think about that for a moment.

When I got married I was happy and very content to be the best
wife and mother I could be. That was my dream and vision...it still
is.... and I was content with that. I had no other big ambitions or
desires.

Then God put a HUGE vision on my heart. Something impossible,
something that said, why me? I can't? I'm not qualified?....

There is a beautiful story written by Max Lucado called "The Oak
inside the Acorn."

The story journeys through the life of an acorn who really doesn't
want to leave Mother Oak, but his mother keeps telling him
*"within you is a great oak tree, Little Acorn. Just be the tree God
made you to be."*

Little Acorn couldn't work out how he was going to be a big Oak,
but slowly and surely this little acorn got buried, became a sapling,
then grew into a Big Oak, and became a significant tree in the life
of a young girl, as it grew up outside her house. One day the little
girl started to worry about her life just like Little Acorn. Little

Acorn, now known as Big Oak, begins to echo to the girl what Mother Oak said to him. *"Within you is a great girl. Just be the person God made you to be."*

As I read this story to my son for the first time one bedtime, I found myself welling up as God reiterated what He was saying to me.

When God puts a God sized vision or dream in your heart that seems impossible, like the acorn you may wonder "how am I going to do this?" Know that in you are all the ingredients to fulfil what has God made you to be.

I realise, looking back, the ingredients for my vision have been seeds within me all along and looking forward He is connecting me with others who have the ingredients I don't have. Put these ingredients together and fuse them with Almighty God and we will see mountains move!

Jesus said, *"Faith as small as a mustard seed (or an acorn) will move mountains."* Wow!

Prayer: *Father God, thank You that You made me unique and perfect. All the ingredients to fulfil my life's purpose are already in me. I choose to join myself with You, for You are the vine and we are Your branches. Let Your life, and Your power flow through me each and every day. I only want to do what I see the Father doing. Give me boldness to step out into my destiny. I know that You are with me and that You will guide me.*

YOUR WORST ENEMY IS NOT THE DEVIL...IT'S YOU!

Victoria Cooper

"For I do not do the good I want to do, but the evil I do not want to do—this I keep on doing. Now if I do what I do not want to do, it is no longer I who do it, but it is sin living in me that does it."
Romans 7:19-20 NIV

I feel like I'm on a constant voyage of self discovery, the older I get the more I realise who I am, who I'm not and what needs to change in me.

Whilst praying and seeking God for breakthrough in a couple of areas of my life I felt the Lord say,

"Your worst enemy in your life is not the devil, it's you."

SAY WHAT?! I wasn't expecting this response.

He went on to say,

"The devil is defeated. I defeated him on the cross. He is not the issue, your flesh is the issue. Your flesh is your enemy, and when you allow your flesh to dominate you, you are giving the devil a foothold into your life."

The Lord then reminded me that my former self died and I'm a new creation. So why am I giving oxygen to my flesh? Galatians 2 says, *"I have been crucified with Christ and I no longer live, but Christ lives in me. The life I now live in the body, I live by faith in the Son of God, who loved me and gave himself for me."* Galatians

2:20 NIV

We are all born with a sinful nature. No one teaches us how to sin, it comes so naturally to us. But even when we "get saved" have you noticed that our transformation to be Christ-like is not immediate?

Yes, our spirits are awakened to God and we are forgiven and filled with His Holy Spirit, but we then have a responsibility to put to death the old man and choose to live by the Spirit.

"So then, brothers and sisters, we have an obligation, but not to our flesh [our human nature, our worldliness, our sinful capacity], to live according to the [impulses of the] flesh [our nature without the Holy Spirit]– for if you are living according to the [impulses of the] flesh, you are going to die. But if [you are living] by the [power of the Holy] Spirit you are habitually putting to death the sinful deeds of the body, you will [really] live forever." Romans 8:12-13 AMP

If we are to see the fullness of what God has for us in our lives it is imperative that we do not allow anything to hold us back in our God given destiny. Yes, the devil will try to thwart God's plans for our lives, but only if we allow him. He waits on the sidelines looking for the open door. He stirs up temptations provoking our old man. But the word of God tells us…

"Submit yourselves, then, to God. Resist the devil, and he will flee from you. Come near to God and he will come near to you." James 4:7-8 NIV

Jesus demonstrated this when he was tempted by the devil in the wilderness in Matthew 4.
You see, God has given us free will. He won't make us do

anything, but He gives us instructions that we have a choice to obey or ignore.

Time and time again the Bible directs us to put to death our old self.

"throw off your old sinful nature and your former way of life, which is corrupted by lust and deception. Instead, let the Spirit renew your thoughts and attitudes. Put on your new nature, created to be like God—truly righteous and holy." Ephesians 4:22-24 NLT

So what are you allowing to dominate you? Fear, unforgiveness, envy, anger, jealousy, gossip? Without realising it we can subtly be feeding our flesh and then wonder why we're struggling. Colossians 3 says,

"But now rid yourselves [completely] of all these things: anger, rage, malice, slander, and obscene (abusive, filthy, vulgar) language from your mouth. Do not lie to one another, for you have stripped off the old self with its evil practices, and have put on the new [spiritual] self who is being continually renewed in true knowledge in the image of Him who created the new self." Col 3:8-10 AMP

God did His part on the cross. We now have a responsibility to do our part. It's not just about saying a one time "yes" to Jesus. Daily we must put to death the old nature in us and choose to renew our mind in the Word of God. Follow His instruction and pledge allegiance to the King of kings.

Prayer: *Jesus, I choose to put my flesh to death, take up my cross daily, and follow You. I thank You that You have made me a new creation! The old has gone, the new has come and I embrace that*

today! I let go of my worries, fear, anxiety, jealousy and unforgiveness, they are my old nature and put on my new nature created to be like You.

DAY 18
LIFT UP HOLY HANDS
Jarrod Cooper

*"He placed the cherubim inside the innermost room of the temple,
with their wings spread out."*
1 Kings 6:27

Raising your hands is such a small thing but can mean so much. I can think of three meanings straight away:

Firstly, if you're being arrested, it's the universal sign for surrender. Be arrested by God today - take a moment to totally surrender everything to Him. Successes and failures, possessions and needs, past and present, hopes and dreams. Our surrender invites Him into our world.

Secondly, if a friend walks towards you with their arms open wide, you know you're in for a loving embrace or a fun bear hug. Let the Father bear hug you today, just like Jesus showed us He does to His lost children in Luke 15:20:

"But while he was still a long way off, his father saw him and was filled with compassion for him; he ran to his son, threw his arms around him and kissed him."

Parental love is perhaps like no other love - It is such a deep, inbuilt, drive of grace, mercy, compassion and desire to see your own children do well. God loves you with exactly that kind of illogical, dangerous, overwhelming parental love. He is overwhelmed with compassion and is going to do all He can do, to see you succeed and know His love.

Let God throw His arms around you today - to surround your heart with the loving embrace of His presence. Soak your mind in the pure, merciful love of God as you remember: *"How great is the Fathers love, that He has lavished on us; that we should be called, children of God! For that is what we are."* (1 John 3:1)

Lastly, scientific studies of the human body have shown that standing up straight, with your face looking slightly upwards, your hands raised and your palms up, is a significant and powerful physical position. The tests have shown that it is very difficult to conjure up any negative emotion when you place your body in such a position.

Amazingly, it is the position of praise!

You were made to praise God because it keeps you emotionally healthy. Why not take some time in a quiet place to stand, raise your hands, and praise Him today?

"I will praise you as long as I live, and in your name I will lift up my hands. I will be fully satisfied as with the richest of foods; with singing lips my mouth will praise you." Psalm 63:4-5

No wonder the cherubim are designed to stand in the presence of God, wings (arms!) permanently lifted to God in worship. I hope that today, our arms would be lifted regularly in surrender, in embrace, in praise and in sacrifice. Surely God will dwell in such a surrendered life.

Action Point: *Raise your arms up to God and spend time worshipping Him and thanking Him today.*

DAY 19
WALK WITH GOD

Jarrod Cooper

"Noah ... walked with God." Genesis 6:9

We often use the phrase *"walking with God"* in a poetic sense - expressing the journey of a life lived God's way. It is a wonderful use of poetry.

But I wonder if that is exactly what the scriptures always mean?

Genesis 3:8 shows us that Adam heard *"the sound of God walking in the cool of the day."* God's Spirit literally moved through the beautiful garden He had planted, seeking out the very reason He made it all in the first place - a place for friendship with man.

It would seem *"walking with God"* in the cool of the evening or the morning was a very real, rather than a metaphorical thing. We might even learn from this, that God loves to be with us as we start and round off our days, walking, chatting, comforting us and empowering us - in the relaxing setting of a mountain, a garden, a quiet walkway.

There is something calming about walking among nature. It soothes our souls, slows our pace, reminds us of the slow beat of seasons and entrances us with the miraculous grace of life. Jesus did it a lot during His ministry. Perhaps there's something in it?

A few weeks ago I lay in bed as my alarm clock swung into action. It felt very, very early. I groaned and turned over in bed thinking, "Oh, I can talk to God in bed this morning, I am so, so tired!"

As I started to chat sleepily to God I had a vivid impression of Jesus standing under the lamp post outside my home, waiting for me. Like a child's friend, asking if another youngster wants to "come out to play" I felt the tug of heaven:

"Come on out! I want to walk with you, to talk with you. I've got some things to share with you. Let's go for a walk."

I resisted for a few seconds, my tired flesh still grumbling louder than the voice of God. But then I relented, pulled on my "early morning clothes" and headed out.

It was as if Jesus was indeed waiting for me, His very best friend (you are that too!), under the lamp post. We walked, we talked, the breath of His Spirit lifted me and stirred my faith, ready for the day ahead.

What a privilege - that Almighty God would call on your house, to see if you want to come out for a walk? What a friendship, what grace, what a kind Father!

Maybe if you turned your ear to heaven right now, you'd hear God say, *"Would you like to go for a walk?*
It really is quite beautiful outside..."

Action Point: *Why not take some time soon, to enjoy a walk with God in the countryside, by a river, or to just sit in a garden or park, and chat to your friend, Jesus?*

DAY 20

GOD'S JIGSAW

Victoria Cooper

"The body is not made up of one part but of many."
1 Corinthians 12:14

I used to love doing jigsaws with my Dad, even if it took days to complete a 1000 piece jigsaw, it was always so satisfying to slot that last piece into place to complete the picture.

However, when a piece went missing it was so frustrating and disappointing to discover the therapeutic hours I'd spent putting this masterpiece together was spoilt by one lost piece. The jigsaw was incomplete and without that last piece the picture was lacking its true beauty.

Life can feel like a jigsaw. A picture bigger than ourselves where we're all connected and each of us has an important part to play.

You may feel that your own life is small and insignificant. Perhaps you struggle to know where you fit in, or perhaps you feel unqualified. You're not sure where you belong or you fear rejection.

In a jigsaw every piece matters and it's the same in the body of Christ.

"I want you to think about how all this makes you more significant, not less. A body isn't just a single part blown up into something huge. It's all the different-but-similar parts arranged and functioning together. As it is, we see that God has carefully placed each part of the body right where he wanted it....The way God

149

designed our bodies is a model for understanding our lives together as a church: every part dependent on every other part, the parts we mention and the parts we don't, the parts we see and the parts we don't. If one part hurts, every other part is involved in the hurt, and in the healing. If one part flourishes, every other part enters into the exuberance." 1 Corinthians 12:14, 25-26 MSG

God has designed us to work as a team. He graces us with various gifts to meet the needs in other people.

I know my own giftings are very limited when I think about the calling on my life, but God has connected me with people who fill those gaps lacking in me and vice versa.

I want to encourage you to step out into the anointing God's placed on your life because you may be the missing gap that fills a void in a church, home group or ministry. Romans 12 says,

"In his grace, God has given us different gifts for doing certain things well. So if God has given you the ability to prophesy, speak out with as much faith as God has given you. If your gift is serving others, serve them well. If you are a teacher, teach well. If your gift is to encourage others, be encouraging. If it is giving, give generously. If God has given you leadership ability, take the responsibility seriously. And if you have a gift for showing kindness to others, do it gladly." Romans 12:6-8 NLT

We have a responsibility to use what God has given us. Even if we feel unqualified, incapable, scared or limited. It's when we step out and obey His voice that God anoints us enabling and gifting us to serve the body of Christ.

You may be the answer to someone else's prayers. It could be your words of encouragement which saves someone's life, or your act of kindness or hospitality which draws people to Jesus. Your hands laid on the sick, your faith engaging in their prayers. Your music which sets people free, your song which releases heaven to earth.

If you don't step into place, we all miss out on the gift God's placed inside of you.
We are all part of God's jigsaw. God connects us and He guides us into place. We just have to obey.

Prayer: *Father God, thank You for the giftings and calling You have placed on my life and even though sometimes I don't feel qualified or able, You qualify me and enable me. I choose to say yes to You today and choose to obey whatever You're asking or calling me to do. Thank you that I am a valuable member of the body of Christ and that You have chosen me.*

A STONE OF HELP

Marion Cooper

"Then Samuel took a stone and set it up between Mizpah and Shen. He named it Ebenezer, saying, "Thus far the Lord has helped us." 1 Samuel 7:12

Every year, I have a little ritual that I enjoy so much. I change all the details and important information in this past year's diary and transfer it into my sparkling next year's diary!

I suppose it's just a little bit like the child beginning a new exercise book in the days of pen and ink, no mistakes, no crossing out, no poor handwriting, no ink blots, just a new fresh beginning. And that is indeed part of my pleasure, a brand New Year lies ahead completely unspoilt and unmarked. What adventures will it hold, what joys and pleasures, what new experiences, what new friends?

But I face every new year having looked back at the old year, because I go through every page of my old diary transferring any relevant information I collected that year, new phone numbers etc. But as I'm looking through for information, I automatically come across all the "happenings" of that year. The dozens of "coffee dates" with dear friends, the days I was booked to look after my gorgeous grandson, the family dinner arrangements. But there are also special church dates, conferences, and half nights of prayer, outreach details, special speakers or indeed dates when I'm out speaking somewhere. There are holiday plans, whether just a brief weekend in the UK or more exciting prolonged trips. Some years there are medical check ups and appointments and sadly, funeral times for loved ones who have died.

As I look back through the year that is just about to close, I feel so many different emotions. Joy and happiness but also a little trepidation at how quickly yet another year has passed. But my overriding emotion is utter and complete gratitude to God for all He has seen me through this last 12 months. Through the ups and downs of life He has kept me, truthfully, He yet again has been my helper.

In 1 Samuel 7.12, Samuel, having defeated the Philistines, took a stone and called it *"Ebenezer,"* which means *"stone of help"* and he said, *"Thus far the Lord has helped me."*

I don't know what past years have held for you, you may have had battles to fight, you may have indeed *'walked through the valley of the shadow of death,'* so as we all enter brand new years ahead, having absolutely no idea what they may hold, we are assured of this one thing, God who has been our Ebenezer, our "stone of help" goes into each new year with us. I can say, God who has been my help as I have walked with Him this last 50+ years, will not fail me in the year to come.

"For He himself has said, "I will never leave you nor forsake you," so we may boldly say, "The Lord is my helper, I will not fear." Hebrews 13.5-6.

Prayer: *Heavenly Father, thank You that You are the Good Shepherd. You lead me beside quiet waters and restore my soul, You prepare a table before me in the presence of my enemies. Your goodness and love chase me all the days of my life. Wherever I go You are with me, You are my helper, my comforter and my guide. I will not fear what is ahead because You are with me.*

DAY 22

BORN OF GOD

Jarrod Cooper

"...Adam, the son of God." Luke 3:38

If you follow the genealogy of Jesus right back, it begins with "Adam, the son of God."

Now Adam was made of mud, (Gen 2:7) but God breathed into the clay corpse of the very first man, and Adam came to life, the son of God.

If today you realise there are great parts of your life that are muddy, clay, dust; then that is good. It's the truth.

But take a moment to meditate on another truth about you:

"For God, who said, "Let light shine out of darkness," made His light shine in our hearts to give us the light of the knowledge of the glory of God in the face of Christ. But we have this treasure in jars of clay to show that this all-surpassing power is from God and not us." 2 Corinthians 4:6-7

In the *"clay jar"* that is your body, there is a treasure (2 Co 4:7). A breath, a divine spark, and it makes you a son of God today; no less God's son than Adam; in fact no less a son than Jesus Himself!

When you came to God in surrender and asked Him into your life, repenting of your sin and asking for His grace - then the Father breathed life into you, just like He did to Adam. The Bible calls it being Born Again, Born of God or Born from Above. A New

Creation came to life when you accepted Jesus!

John 3:6 says, *"Flesh gives birth to flesh, but the Spirit gives birth to spirit. You should not be surprised at my saying "You must be born again."*

When your fleshly mother gave birth, you were "born of flesh." But when you accepted Jesus into your life, you were born a second time, from above, as God's Spirit gave birth to a new person, Christ in you! You became a new creation, literally, a new species. You are now a child of God, the old has gone, the new has come!

Why not take a moment to let the Spirit of God breathe into your life again today? That wonderful Spirit will *"testify to your spirit that you are His child"* (Romans 8:16). In fact, a cry will rise up from within you *"Abba, Daddy, Father"* (Romans 8:15) - and you will remember that you are not simply a child of this earth, but a child of God; loved, forgiven, cared for, an overcomer!

Your Father is going to help you through everything today - so be strong!

Prayer: *Abba, Father, Daddy, thank You for making me Your child. You have clothed me in royal robes I don't deserve. A garment of righteousness. You have crowned me with splendour. A royal diadem in Your hands. I linger in Your presence without inferiority, guilt or condemnation. Jesus, because of You I am holy, blameless and free.*

A MAN JUST LIKE US

Jarrod Cooper

"Elijah was a man just like us." James 5:17

We would love to think people who move in miracles, claim to hear God's voice clearly and fulfill great destinies, are people that are somehow wired completely differently to us.

When we see impressive people I wonder if we're tempted to think, *"They probably float dreamily in a heavenly encounter every night. They glow. They feel good all the time. They perspire sweet aromas and never lose their tempers."*

Well, the truth is, God always has and always will use very normal people just like you and me. People who lose it, have bad hair days and who don't always know if they're "doing it right!" People who get depressed, feel fakes, have fears, weaknesses, relational fallouts and sin occasionally.

Elijah bravely confronted hundreds of enemies and saw God move powerfully. But then he got terrified of one woman, and ended depressed and suicidal in an embarrassing pity-party! The same is true of most of our biblical heroes: Noah got drunk, Jacob was a deceiver, Joseph was a show-off, Moses stammered, David was a moral failure, Solomon was wise but full of lust, Thomas was a doubter, Paul got into terrible arguments and Peter struggled with fear on and off throughout his whole life.

Yet this list of people had God's ear, saw God transform their worlds, they shaped history with God's help and learned to grasp His grace even in the midst of their brokenness.

The glory of the Gospel is simply this: God takes broken and failing humans, and makes them remarkable!

He adds His "super" to our "natural" and we become supernatural. He adds His "extra" to our "ordinary" and we become extraordinary.

In fact, have you ever thought, that in some ways, your weaknesses actually qualify you for salvation by grace? The whole reason He died, is so that He could show off His incredible love and power by making something glorious out of your brokenness! All you have to do is trust Him!

"Because of His great love for us, God, who is rich in mercy, made us alive with Christ ... it is by grace you have been saved ... through faith, it is the gift of God - not by works, so that no-one can boast." Ephesians 2:4,8

Let's drop the feeble excuse in our heads, that all our spiritual heroes have some heritage that sets them apart. Some unattainable secret that we could never find. You have His presence, His word and His voice. That means you have access to all the resources and power of God - stop focusing on your failings and start enjoying His presence, knowing His word and listening to His voice. That is ALL you need to live an extraordinary supernatural life, that turns the world upside down for the purposes of God!

Prayer: *Thank You God that I am saved by grace. Thank You I am Your work of art and You are working in me to will and to do according to Your good pleasure. I renew my faith today, that Your mercy forgives me, Your presence empowers me, and I will live a supernatural life, by the Grace of God upon me!*

DRINK DEEPLY OF GOD'S KINDNESS

Jarrod Cooper

"Drink deeply of God's pure kindness" 2 Peter 2:2 *(The Message)*

1 John 4:18 tells us *"there is no fear in love"* and that *"He who fears has not been made perfect in love."*

The existence (or not) of fear is the barometer of our level of acceptance of God's Love. The more you realise the power of His love and how it is directed at your life personally, the less you will fear.

We may find it easy to believe in a theoretical God of love. But that will count little unless we are completely convinced that His love is for us, personally.

In order for His love to land in your life, let me work through one thought with you. Answer this question for me, "Why do you exist?"

I know you are not an accident. Even if your parents did not "plan you," God is so infinitely great that He sits outside of time (as well as within it!), so He sees the end from the beginning, and has had you in mind before the world began. You are no mistake - you were birthed with a purpose! If in doubt, read Psalm 139 right now.

So if you are not an accident, then still I ask, why are you here? Does God need your help? Is He some frustrated powerless divine figure, trying to get men to join His plan of looking after the planet? Of course not!

God is all-powerful, self-sufficient, all-knowing and omni-present. He does not need you and I to get a thing done, ever!

So, is it that God wants something or someone to take His wrath out upon? No! He IS love!

Having exhausted all possible explanations for our existence, I am left with one, life-changing conclusion: God made you for one reason, and one reason alone - He made you to love you.

The only reason we exist is for our loving Father to pour out His love upon us! He wants to enjoy us, to fellowship with us, to dance with us and walk with us. Half the time I don't even like myself, but He absolutely adores me! When we understand this, our lives are utterly transformed.

So, when your thoughts are resistant to the overwhelming ocean of God's grace, take all the guilty, religious, pseudo-holy thoughts captive. Push beyond dull religion and take one extra dangerous step to dive into the depth of His love by saying to yourself; *"No, today, I am going to believe He completely adores me. Like a Father to a Son, I am the apple of His eye. His love is not dependent on my actions, but on my lineage. I am His child - and He unconditionally loves me."*

Nothing will cause you to live fearlessly, righteously, uncompromisingly, like drinking deeply of God's kindness. It's the holiest thing you could do!

Action Point: *Take some moments to meditate on the love of God for you while reading Psalm 139.*

DAY 25

WINTER

Jarrod Cooper

"As soon as I send Artemas or Tychicus to you, do your best to come to me at Nicopolis, because I have decided to winter there." (Titus 3:12 NIV)

In this passage Paul is sailing on his mission, and says he is going to "winter" in Nicopolis away from the worst of the bad winter-time weather.

These days it is possible and normal to travel anywhere, almost any time. However there was a time when trips across the sea were best taken at certain times; the weather could halt your plans for a whole season. While seasons may not often stop us travelling anymore naturally speaking, spiritually we need to retain the art of reading the seasons of our destiny correctly and "wintering" at the right time.

In our fast paced, pressured lives, endlessly seeking signs of success and fruitfulness, we can lose the balance of wintering, of slowing down, taking some time from the "front-line," of protecting ourselves from inclement weather and using that time to replenish spirit, soul & body.

The Bible is full of pictures of rest and seasons of recuperation. It is powerful and very important. To not understand it is to be idolatrous in regards our own strengths.

The Bible speaks of Sabbaths; Sabbath days, even Sabbath years. It speaks of leaving fields fallow, as it allows the soil to replenish its mineral nourishment. It speaks of pruned branches, of waiting on the Lord. It shows that inactivity is as important as activity. Not doing is as godly as doing. Rest is presented, not as a second class use of time, but an act of worship.

Several years ago God began to speak to me about wintering, taking a season of lessened pressure. I didn't quite know how to do this, as I'm a busy person, so I procrastinated for a while. But one Sunday, as one of our leaders led a prayer meeting, I distinctly heard them prophecy loudly "Winter, winter, winter!"

It was a strange thing for this leader to say, and they may never know what God was doing, but God arrested my spirit as he spoke, and I knew I had to respond. For a year I adjusted my diary to increase my prayer and lessen high stress activities. I did more in hiding, and less high profile appointments. To some, I dropped off the map.

In that time my intimacy with God increased and I had amazing revelations of His protection. I became more centered, more sensitive to Him, more refreshed and replenished. But also in this time, storms and trials blew through several things our church was doing - but from my internal posture of "wintering," the trials had little effect on me. God had warned me, and so I was ready to "hide in Him."

Read the seasons of life. Know when to push on and when to rest. Know when to rise and when to happily sit in obscurity. Know how to be recognised and how to be overlooked. Discover how to be good at busyness, and outstanding at rest. Be fruitful, but also be fallow. Both are healthy parts of a good life.

Meditate today, and embrace the winter when it comes.

Prayer: *Lord give me Your wisdom to read well the seasons of my life; when to rise up and when to rest.*

I FOUND MYSELF BEFORE GOD

Victoria Cooper

"You are altogether beautiful, my darling! There is no blemish in you!" Song of songs 4:7

I can't figure out if it was a vision or a dream, but some time ago I found myself before my Heavenly Father. He said He was pleased with me and thanked me for things I'd done and said.

I kept apologising for all the wrong things I had done and things I shouldn't have said. Things I didn't do very well and situations I could have handled better.

God wouldn't acknowledge what I was saying, it was like He couldn't hear me, He was ignoring me.

I went on and on but He would just respond with all the good things I'd done. I got frustrated waiting for a response to my apology until He eventually said, *"as far as the east is from the west, I have removed your sin. I dealt with this on the cross, so why are you bringing it up?"*

"He has removed our sins as far from us as the east is from the west." Psalm 103:12 NLT

We can be so aware of our humanity that we forget the incredible gift from God that makes us holy and acceptable to Him. The New Testament repeatedly speaks of the pardoning of our sins through Jesus, reconciling us to God.

"But you were washed [by the atoning sacrifice of Christ], you

were sanctified [set apart for God, and made holy], you were justified [declared free of guilt] in the name of the Lord Jesus Christ and in the [Holy] Spirit of our God [the source of the believer's new life and changed behavior]." 1 Corinthians 6:11 AMP

Notice, these scriptures are past tenses.
"He has removed our sins." "You were washed....you were sanctified...... You were justified."

It's already done. We are clean. Our sins have been deleted, erased, eliminated, eradicated, abolished, by the powerful blood of Jesus. Praise God!

But like me in my vision, do you ever feel the need to highlight your mistakes or do you struggle to believe God can forgive others but not you?

Do you ever feel like the Apostle Paul when he writes; *"And I know that nothing good lives in me, that is, in my sinful nature. I want to do what is right, but I can't. I want to do what is good, but I don't. I don't want to do what is wrong, but I do it anyway. But if I do what I don't want to do, I am not really the one doing wrong; it is sin living in me that does it." Romans 7:18-20 NLT*

Or perhaps your response when God "turns up" in a meeting is like Simon Peter; *"Oh, Lord, please leave me—I'm too much of a sinner to be around you." Luke 5:8 NLT*

God knows we are but dust, broken weak vessels, born into sin.

"The LORD is like a father to his children, tender and compassionate to those who fear him. For he knows how weak we are; he remembers we are only dust." Psalm 103:13-14 NLT

Yet because of Jesus we are not only forgiven, but when we accept Him into our lives, we carry Him. Like the colt which He rode into Jerusalem on before He was sent to the cross. He chooses the weak, and the fragile to emanate His glory.

"For God, who said, "Let light shine out of darkness," is the One who has shone in our hearts to give us the Light of the knowledge of the glory and majesty of God [clearly revealed] in the face of Christ. But we have this precious treasure [the good news about salvation] in [unworthy] earthen vessels [of human frailty], so that the grandeur and surpassing greatness of the power will be [shown to be] from God [His sufficiency] and not from ourselves." 2 Corinthians 4:6-7 AMP

So recognise this amazing transaction God did by sending His Son. Accept it, receive it and step into the fullness of God's blessings.

Start seeing yourself as God sees you. You're loved by Him, you're forgiven....
"...you are a chosen people. You are royal priests, a holy nation, God's very own possession. As a result, you can show others the goodness of God, for he called you out of the darkness into his wonderful light." 1 Peter 2:9 NLT

If you still struggle to accept God's forgiveness, speak the following verse over your life and repeat each day until you believe it and receive it.

Confession of faith: *"My old self has been crucified with Christ. It is no longer I who live, but Christ lives in me. So I live in this earthly body by trusting in the Son of God, who loved me and gave himself for me." Galatians 2:20 NLT*

ARE YOU BROKEN?
Jarrod Cooper

"My sacrifice O God, is a broken spirit; a broken and contrite heart, O God, you will not despise." Psalm 51:17

Every year, in Great Britain, we hold Remembrance Sunday, when we honour those who have died for our freedom in the many wars our world has endured. I find the words of Jim Radford's "The Shores of Normandy" so moving, as they tell his story of being a young galley boy among that amazing fleet that went to confront our enemies on the 6th June 1944. One verse says…

Now the Empire Larch was a deep-sea tug with a crew of thirty-three,
And I was just the galley-boy on my first trip to sea.
I little thought when I left home of the dreadful sights I'd see,
But I came to manhood on the day that I first saw Normandy.

He sings of men dying among the swirling tides of Normandy. And on that day, seeing the horrors of war as a 15 year old lad, he became a man. He saw the brokenness of the world in all its pain, sorrow and grief and it became a moment of transformation.

In many ways we all grow up to adulthood when we are touched by the brokenness of the world, and also when we travel through our own personal seasons of pain. At times we are broken through the cruelty of others, or through the pains of this world in sickness and death. Sometimes we break ourselves against the rocks of sin and shame. Whichever way it comes, most discover the pain of brokenness sooner or later.

Perhaps as you read this, you are broken, in pain, confused, overwhelmed, crushed.

The good news is, God is still with you.

And God is still for you.

And there is life after brokenness.

Isaiah 57:15 says, *"For this is what the high and lofty One says-- he who lives forever, whose name is holy: "I live in a high and holy place, but also with him who is broken and lowly in spirit, to revive the spirit of the lowly and to revive the heart of the contrite."*

To be broken means to be smashed, crushed, torn, shattered, crouched down. Is that you today?

King David was crushed by the shame and disillusionment of his own sin. He'd committed adultery, then had the woman's husband killed. This special king, who was remarkably called a *"man after God's own heart"* had failed, and failed hugely. He was broken, shattered, ruined - devastated by his own wickedness and selfishness.

But in Psalm 51, the song where he confesses his sin and pain, he draws to the end saying, *"My sacrifice O God, is a broken spirit; a broken and contrite heart, O God, you will not despise."*

I'm sure there had been times when he had brought God a more excited, passionate, glorious worship. But today, it was his brokenness that became his sacrifice. He gave God his crushed spirit, his torn emotions, his overwhelmed mind, his shattered heart. He turned his brokenness into a sacrifice of worship.

So, broken friend - God does not despise that tear soaked broken worship. In fact, He will receive it, and in return wash you with grace, mercy, healing and wholeness; a divine exchange – Beauty for ashes. Glory for suffering. Dancing for mourning.

Worship God with your brokenness today. Let him turn your brokenness into beauty. It may be the purest worship you've ever brought.

Prayer: *Jesus, thank You that You have washed me and I am now clean. You have cancelled my sins, wiped them out and declared me not guilty. You take my sorrow and shame and exchange it for joy and righteousness. I worship You, for You are good and Your love endures forever.*

DON'T LET IT GET UNDER YOUR SKIN

Victoria Cooper

"The thief comes only to steal and kill and destroy; I have come that they may have life, and have it to the full." John 10:10 NIV

Do you ever have those days or weeks where there's not one problem bothering you, but several?

The car breaks down, the boiler stops working. Family members get sick, children winding you up, unexpected bills to pay....

It's like those crazy gnats that follow you in the woods when you're trying to take a pleasant walk on a sunny afternoon, and they completely ruin the whole idyllic experience.

Or like those tiny houses flies that buzz around your face, taunting you, happy to have taken up residency in your house plants.

These are small irritations, pests that can, if we let them, drive us crazy, send our blood pressure soaring and cause us headaches.

Did you know, one of the names for the devil is *"Lord of the Flies?"*

He comes and wears us down with irritations, he seeks to take away our God given peace, erodes our passion, drains our strength and exhausts our emotions....If we let him.

Flies are never going to go away, (unfortunately) and neither is the devil. This is why we need to recognise the enemies tactics. John 10 says,

"The thief comes only to steal and kill and destroy; I have come that they may have life, and have it to the full." John 10:10 NIV

The Devil comes to steal (our peace), kill our joy, (that which gives us strength (Neh 8:10)) and destroy (our day).

Nothing major has to happen for the devil to take from our lives. Just lots of small, irritating mole hills that can be turned into mountains within our minds.

Don't take the bait that he waves in front of you. He wants you to react with fear and frustration instead of trust and confidence. Don't let him distract you from what's important.

So choose to keep your peace, don't lose your joy and don't let the devil have a foothold. (Eph 4:27)

Don't let him get under your skin. If you do.....well, I'll let you google what happens when flies get under the skin.

Prayer: *I thank You Father God that I can overcome the devil because Jesus dwells within me. No weapon formed against me will prosper. I allow Your peace to take control of my body, soul and mind as I choose to fix my eyes on You, the Author and Perfecter of my faith.*

DAY 29
COCKROACHES
Marion Cooper

"Finally, brothers and sisters, whatever is true, whatever is noble, whatever is right, whatever is pure, whatever is lovely, whatever is admirable—if anything is excellent or praiseworthy—think about such things." Philippians 4:8

When our family were living and working in Gibraltar, one Spring my husband and I drove to a ministers and missionary conference in Madrid. Because the conference ended fairly late in the day, it was necessary for us to break our journey home and spend a night in a hotel.

We were in the mountains south of Madrid, when we found an isolated hotel and drove in to spend the night. The receptionist took us up stairs to show us our room and I did vaguely note that he turned on the bathroom light but showed us the bedroom first. It wasn't the Ritz but it was clean enough and it was only for one night and there was no other hotel anyway, so we took the room.

All seemed well, we went down to the restaurant for a little dinner then, very weary, went to bed. It was during the night that I heard my husband go to the bathroom, shortly followed by a very girly scream! Alarmed, I called out, *"What's the matter?"*

"I wish I hadn't done that! It was horrific! Every surface was covered in cockroaches and as I turned on the light they scuttled away into their holes!" he moaned.

Needless to say we spent the rest of the night with the bathroom light on; we didn't want those cockroaches feeling they could resume their wanderings while we were there.

Now bad, negative thoughts are just like cockroaches, they come out in the dark. Sometimes I find I am a strong woman of God all day, then during the night those negative thoughts assume massive proportions and disturb my sleep. You know what those thoughts are like, fearful, anxious thoughts, financial worries, doubts, concerns and cares, health worries, worry for our families, our children, the church, the nation even.

Whether these thoughts come literally in the night or just when we are in a "dark" place we can send them scuttling back into their holes by shining the light of God's word on them. Give them no place in our minds.

To defeat these negative thoughts, read His word, meditate on it, declare it, memorize it, repeat it to yourself.

Psalm 119:105 says, *"Your word is a lamp to my feet and a light to my path."*

Prayer: *Thank You Lord that You are always with me. Even in the darkest of nights, Your light shines through, penetrating my night. Your word is a light to my path and I choose to let it shine in every area of my life. I renew my mind on Your word and choose to think and dwell on Your goodness, Your faithfulness, Your righteousness, Your Peace and take comfort in knowing my life rests in Your hands.*

DAY 30
THERE'S GOODNESS IN THE GUNK
Victoria Cooper

"As for you, you meant evil against me, but God meant it for good." Genesis 50:20

Joseph went through a tough time.

He went from being favourite son to a slave, favoured by Potiphar to prisoner. He was a man of dreams. A man of discernment who knew His God.

"The Lord was with Joseph so that he prospered, and he lived in the house of his Egyptian master. When his master saw that the Lord was with him and that the Lord gave him success in everything he did...." Genesis 39:2-3

When God's favour is on you, when He gives you dreams and you walk in His ways, I guarantee this will attract envy, jealousy and other demonic opposition.

But whatever was thrown at Joseph to bring him down, God used it to take him to the next level, which led Joseph to a place far above and beyond his expectations.

From prisoner to Prime Minister.

Recently I planted a large shrub in my garden. I had to dig a hole twice as big as it's pot, then once planted, I filled the hole with a special compost which contained a mixture of fresh rotten organic matter and manure.

To my eyes (and nose), it was horrible, gunky, rotting dead stuff and poo! Nothing special about it....it was gross!!

But I can tell you today. That shrub is thriving.

There's goodness in the gunk!

Sometimes you have got to go through some "gunk"... "rubbish"... "poo" (whatever you want to call it), to get you to where God wants you to be.

Like this shrub and like Joseph you may feel like you're in a hole with a load of manure thrown on you. Broken relationships, hurtful conversations, spiteful words, lost dreams, betrayals, deaths, lies and disappointments.

Let them be the ultimate compost that catapult you to far beyond your wildest dreams.

Don't let it make you bitter, let it make you better. Don't let it dwell in your heart, place it under your feet, let it bring nourishment to your roots and let it make you stronger.

Even in his darkest hour, Joseph kept his heart clean and trusted God to look after him.

"Joseph's master took him and put him in prison, the place where the king's prisoners were confined. But while Joseph was there in the prison, the Lord was with him; he showed him kindness and granted him favour in the eyes of the prison warden." Genesis 39:20 NIV

God will honour you and He will vindicate you.

Trust Him and He will lift you out of the pit (Ps 40), and place royal robes on your shoulders (Gen 41:42).

Then perhaps you can look at your brothers and sisters and say, *"you meant evil against me, but God meant it for good"* Gen 50:20.

Prayer: *Father, help me to keep my heart pure and right before You, even when I go through hurtful situations. I choose to forgive those who have hurt me and allow You to heal my heart. I trust You to make all things work together for my good knowing You have my best interests at heart. Help me to allow this process to make me a better person and not a bitter person. I cast all my cares upon You knowing You care for me.*

THE GOD WHO SEES ME
Jarrod Cooper

Hagar gave this name to the Lord who spoke to her: "You are the God who sees me," for she said, "I have now seen the One who sees me." Genesis 16:13 NIV

Hagar was an outcast, wandering in a desert, caught in the storm of a moral maze. She was an Egyptian slave and the mother of Abraham's *"son of unbelief,"* Ishmael.

Used unnecessarily to try to give birth to Abraham's heir (because his wife was barren), Hagar was subsequently mistreated and despised; she eventually found herself in a lonely, difficult, tangled circumstance.

Taking her young son, she ran away from the very family who caused the moral mess, and is soon found wandering in a desert, thirsty and alone. Leaving her son crying under a bush in the desert to die, she began to sob too. Then God stepped in ...

"God heard the boy crying, and the angel of the Lord called Hagar from heaven ... "Do not be afraid Hagar, God has heard the boy crying... I will make him a great nation."

There, in the desert of loss and confusion, God finds her, and she gives Jehovah the name: *"You are the God who sees me."*

Realise today, it doesn't matter who you are, what moral failure, what crippling trial, what confusing circumstance or hope-sapping depression you are in - God sees you.

He sees it all, knows it all, gathers all your tears in a jar and weeps alongside you. In fact, He is still committed to picking your life up and turning your burden into a blessing, your trial into a testimony and your sin into splendour, if you call to Him.

Psalm 139:5 says, *"You hem me in behind and before, and you lay your hand upon me."* That means He surrounds you, covering your yesterdays, shielding your today and stands waiting in your tomorrow. Everything that seems confusing today, He promises to turn to good. Just keep trusting.

"Trust in the Lord with all your heart, lean not on your own understanding, in all your ways acknowledge Him, and He will make your paths straight." Proverbs 3:5

That means if we simply control the raging thoughts of anxiety within, and instead commit our thoughts to trusting His good kindness, He will construct a super-highway beneath our feet. He will build a way out for us. Of that we can be certain. And like Hagar you will say, *"I have seen the God who sees me."*

See that He's right there, at your right hand, watching over you. He will never leave you, nor forsake you, ever.

Prayer: *Thank You Jesus that You are for me, not against me. You see me right now, and know everything I am going through. I commit myself to trust You in my mind and my heart, believing You will build a highway under my feet.*

DAY 32
HE WHO DWELLS WILL REST
Jarrod Cooper

"He who dwells in the secret place of the most high God, will rest in the shadow of the Almighty." Psalm 91:1

Do you want to find true rest for your soul today? Not leisure, distraction or numbness - but actual, pure, peaceful - rest? Then simply confess everything you know in you that is offensive to God and His word. Ask Him to help you "turn away" from it (that's called repentance).

Acts 3:19 puts it this way, *"Repent, then, and turn to God, so that your sins may be wiped out, that times of refreshing may come from the Lord."*

Next, receive all the grace and forgiveness bought for you through the Cross, forgiving yourself for failing too.

1 John 1:9 promises, *"If we confess our sins, He is faithful and just and will forgive us our sins and purify us from all unrighteousness."*

Psalms 103:2-3 states, *"Forget not all His benefits ... who forgives all your sins."* while verse 10 says *"He will not treat us as our sins deserve."*

Hebrews 8:12 ensures us, *"I will remember their sins no more"* while 2 Corinthians 5:19 firmly declares He is commited to *"...not counting mens sins against them."*
All these verses assure you of complete and total forgiveness. You never need to bring up old sins, God has already chosen to forget

them, at the very moment you confessed them!

Now you're ready to dwell in His secret place. Simply make a choice to be completely relaxed and settled in the presence of God right now. Imagine Him in you, and you in Him.

Settle your heart in His love. Slow your thoughts down and focus on the grace of Jesus. Simply "be" in the presence of God. Don't think of the future - simply be present, now.

Can you sense a secret place of presence inside you now? A gentle stirring of God's grace, mercy and quiet, loving communion? A sense of peace, of approval, of safety, of quiet awe?

This is *"The secret place of the Most High God."*

Dwell there, day in, day out. Return to it if you forget, night or day. Practice that presence - and you will increasingly discover a life filled with the deep breath of heaven's rest.

You see, He who dwells in the secret place, will rest.

Action Point: *Practice confessing all sin, all worry and giving all cares to God. Then receive His forgiveness and forgive yourself too. Then be quiet in His presence, thanking Him for His grace and asking Him to fill you with His Spirit.*

SPRING IS JUST AROUND THE CORNER

Victoria Cooper

"See! The winter is past; the rains are over and gone. Flowers appear on the earth; the season of singing has come, the cooing of doves is heard in our land. The fig tree forms its early fruit; the blossoming vines spread their fragrance. Arise, come, my darling; my beautiful one, come with me."
Song of Songs 2:11-13 NIV

Spring, the season where it seems that everything comes back to life.

Wonderful! I love those seasons, but have you ever felt like your Spring season is taking ages to come around?

I remember walking through a country village and all around me the leaves were bursting through, flowers blossoming, grass growing, but there was this one tree which hadn't burst into leaf yet. It wasn't dead, but it still looked like it was in its winter.

At the time I had been through a tough season. I felt depleted and I remember saying to my husband, *"I feel just like that tree."* Everyone else was enjoying their "Spring" and moving forward into all God has for them and I felt stuck in my "Winter."

The tree was an Oak. It's usually one of the last trees to burst into leaf. During the Winter months, the Oak draws all it's nutrients into it's root system and stores them to survive the next season. It may appear fruitless and bare but all of it's goodness is stored deep in it's roots ready to burst into the next season.
Like the Oak...Don't despise the winter seasons in your life. This is

a time to draw back, preserve, take stock, and rest in God's presence, before you push into your next season. The Oak is a symbol of strength, endurance and survival. It produces one of the hardest and most durable timbers in the world, but it takes many years before an oak is ready for construction.

If you're in a "winter" season know that there is a reason. God is making you strong. Put your roots in Him and soak in His presence. Take time to read and absorb His word. Don't let this season get you down. Endure it, because your "Spring" is just around the corner.

God knows what He's doing. We can not rush His timings and seasons.

"There is a season (a time appointed) for everything and a time for every delight and event or purpose under heaven." Ecc 3:1 AMP

So be strong you mighty "oak of righteousness." For He will...

"bestow on you a crown of beauty instead of ashes, the oil of joy instead of mourning, and a garment of praise instead of a spirit of despair. You will be called oaks of righteousness, a planting of the Lord for the display of his splendour." Isaiah 61:3 NIV

God's not finished with you yet.

Action Point: *Take some time to meditate on the word of God. Choose one of the scriptures above or one of your favourite verses. Read it in different versions. Draw strength from His word to you today.*

DAY 34
MAKE REST PART OF YOUR WORK
Victoria Cooper

"Come to me, all who are weary and burdened, and I will give you rest." Matthew 11:28

I like to get things done. I have a mind mentality of planning, writing lists and ticking things off. It's how I operate. But God stopped me in my tracks recently and said. *"Make rest part of your work."*

I work from home. I have the hours of the school day whilst my son is at school, to get everything I need to do, done. Every minute is precious, I dare not waste a second.....yet God asks me to make rest part of my work?! Unfortunately this would sit at the bottom of my "to do" list.

In a UK survey 43% believe they have too much work to take a rest, with many eating lunch at their desk whilst responding to emails. Having recently meditated on the scripture in Hebrews 4, I am starting to realise how much God takes rest seriously.

"God's promise of entering his rest still stands, so we ought to tremble with fear that some of you might fail to experience it. Hebrews 4:1 NLT

From the moment of creation God introduced and demonstrated rest and followed it up with the 10 commandments.

"You have six days each week for your ordinary work, but the seventh day is a Sabbath day of rest dedicated to the LORD your God....For in six days the LORD made the heavens, the earth, the

sea, and everything in them; but on the seventh day he rested. That is why the LORD blessed the Sabbath day and set it apart as holy." Exodus 20:9-11 NLT

When you love your work, you probably don't see the need to rest. Alternatively you may feel overwhelmed with the amount of work you have to do (especially if you work full time, and you have a house and family to look after). Either way, we are in danger of making work idolatrous. I'm often reminded of the story of Mary and Martha.

"Mary, who sat before the Master, hanging on every word he said. But Martha was pulled away by all she had to do in the kitchen. Later, she stepped in, interrupting them. "Master, don't you care that my sister has abandoned the kitchen to me? Tell her to lend me a hand." The Master said, "Martha, dear Martha, you're fussing far too much and getting yourself worked up over nothing. One thing only is essential, and Mary has chosen it." Luke 10:38-42 MSG

We have to CHOOSE rest.

There is always going to be "something" to do, whether it be emails to write, clothes to iron or people to see. Let's make sure REST is near the top of our "to do" list and make rest part of our work.

Prayer: *Forgive me Father God when I have chosen what I want to do rather than what You want me to do. When I have taken the burden on to myself rather than giving it to You. I want to operate in Your strength, not my own. Forgive me for striving and help me to rest, rest in Your presence, rest in Your promises, rest in Your word.*

DISCOVER SELF DISCIPLINE
Jarrod Cooper

"Without a vision the people cast off restraint" Proverbs 29:18

Ever felt a failure because you lack the discipline others seem to have? While others have disciplined prayer lives, diets, spending habits or exercise regimes - you just can't seem to work up that will power! It's so frustrating.

It will make you unhappy too, because people who lack self-discipline are never happy with themselves.

But there is a secret to discipline. It is true that some are simply wired to think in disciplined patterns more naturally than others. Some have learned certain disciplines by practiced behaviour. But there is a third secret to discipline that just may help you:

Discipline comes from vision.

Get a vision, and you'll become disciplined - without even thinking that you are!

People with a vision get out of bed thinking about the vision. They pray to fulfil the vision. They seek God because they need His help. They save money, get fit, give up time or leisure or even change their diet because they have a vision.

The hope that springs from vision, will spark disciplines and restraints in you, that you never thought possible.

You see, without a vision we *"cast off restraint"* the NIV version of the Bible says. That means that purpose puts power and healthy restraints in our lives. We live better, if we are living with purpose.

The New Living Translation says that purposeless people *"run wild,"* while The Message version says that visionless people *"stumble all over themselves."*

It is clear that vision, purpose and calling release us into a new kind of living. In fact, most of the frustrations young Christians have with their spiritual maturity is simply because they are lacking purpose. It is impossible to live the Christian life well, without knowing the reason for that Christian life. To *"live a life worthy of the call"* (Eph 4:1) you must know that call!

Knowing God's call comes from listening to His voice or from serving and experimenting with purpose in our church teams. It also comes from knowing what excites us and what angers us (There are things we are born to change, so we feel passion and frustration about them).

All these point to God's purpose. And once His purpose begins to burn in our souls, we become unstoppable!

Action Point: *Is it time to seek God for a new or clearer sense of God's purpose in your life? One great way to do this is to get a paper and pen and begin to write out what you think God might say to you about who you are, why you were born and what He wants you to do in life. Ask God to speak as you write, then meditate and ponder the results.*

FROM AVERAGE TO "A" GRADES
Victoria Cooper

"The Lord searches all the earth for people who have given themselves completely to him." *2 Chronicles 16:9 NCV*

The revivalist D.L. Moody once heard a preacher say, *"The world has yet to see what God can do with a man fully surrendered to Him."* Moody that night said, *"By God's grace I'll be that man!"*

I was a fairly average student at school. Never brilliant at anything specific..... just OK. I'm not trying to be super humble here. I simply never reached the "A" grade I always worked hard for.

The quote above from D.L. Moody truly resonated with me from a young age and I remember thinking, if I gave my myself completely to God, He could turn all my averages into A grades, and God has not disappointed me. As I have given God my abilities and availability He has far exceeded my expectations.

When God told Moses to tell Pharaoh to let the Israelites go, Moses questioned God, he knew it was beyond his capability. Yet God's response was, *"what's in your hand?"*

"Moses answered, "What if they do not believe me or listen to me and say, 'The Lord did not appear to you'?" Then the Lord said to him, "What is that in your hand?" "A staff," he replied. The Lord said, "Throw it on the ground." Exodus 4:1-3 NIV

God used the very tool that was in Moses' hand and God partnered with Him as Moses obeyed the Lord.

I promise you, as you lay down at God's feet what is in your hand......your gifts, talents, skills, however good or average. He'll far exceed your expectations too.

It's a fusion of humanity and divinity.

You see, God wants to partner with us, He's not looking for perfect people. He's looking for the "has nots" and the "should nots" to display His glory through.

"But God chose the foolish things of the world to shame the wise; God chose the weak things of the world to shame the strong. God chose the lowly things of this world and the despised things—and the things that are not—to nullify the things that are, so that no one may boast before him." 1 Corinthians 1:27-29 NIV

As my husband often says,
"Acts of obedience release the power of God in our lives" - Jarrod Cooper

You may not think you have much to offer. You may feel weak, incapable, untalented....

PERFECT! This means you qualify.

Gideon was the least in his family and part of the weakest clan (Judges 6:15).
Jeremiah was young (Jeremiah 1:7).
Abraham was old (Genesis 18:11).
Jonah was afraid and ran away (Jonah 1).
David was overlooked by his family, but God was looking, searching for a man after God's own heart, and David went from being a shepherd boy to being a King.

"I've searched the land and found this David, son of Jesse. He's a

man whose heart beats to my heart, a man who will do what I tell him." Acts 13:22 MSG

Don't let excuses get in the way of God's purpose for your life. Don't disqualify yourself.

Step out and give yourself completely to Him because He's looking for your availability not your ability.

Prayer: *Father God, enlighten my eyes to know Your hope, Your inheritance for me and Your incomparably great power available to me today. I give You my hopes, my dreams, my gifts and my talents and I lay them at Your feet. I choose to align myself with You and ask You to use what I have for the glory of Your Kingdom.*

HOW'S YOUR HEART?
Victoria Cooper

"Above all else, guard your heart, for everything you do flows from it."
Proverbs 4:23 NIV

How's your heart? Not your physical, pumping heart inside your rib cage...No, I'm talking about the centre of your being. The real inner you.

I have to be honest and say sometimes my heart can feel a bit like my imac computer....

It used to be so slow that I'd leave it to chunter away whilst I went to do the laundry or hang out the washing. I'd turn it on in the mornings 10 minutes before I needed to use it so I didn't have to sit there and watch it loading.

Now, I'm no "techie-kind-a-person" but I do know that when this happens, there's too much going on for the computer to cope with, unnecessary programs running in the background and it needs a serious clean up and "de-frag" (or whatever you call it).

When we don't keep our hearts clean and guarded from irritations, accusations, gossip, hurts, jealousy and insecurity, then like my imac computer we struggle to operate effectively and become weary. Too much is going on on the inside of us for our hearts to cope with. I believe this can delay our destiny and even put our lives on hold.

Perhaps, (like with me and my computer) God's waiting for us to "load" and goes to do other work or use someone else until we're ready to cooperate?

Ouch!! My heart immediately cries, *"Don't pass me by! I want to be ready to be used by You."*

As I've been reading the story of David in the Bible, I am overwhelmed by his heart-response to many situations he faced. He was not only a man after God's own heart but he was a man who knew how to guard his heart. He was pursued with hate, envy and jealousy by King Saul, a man David served and honoured.

Many times David asked the question, (talking to Jonathan, Saul's son)

"What have I done? What is my crime? How have I wronged your father, that he is trying to kill me?" 1 Samuel 20:1

Twice David had the opportunity to kill him but he chose to show honour. He never avenged himself, even when he had the opportunity.

"I will not lay my hand on my lord, because he is the Lord's anointed." 1 Samuel 24:10

David's heart was kept humble, pure and dependant on God. In Psalm 119 he writes,

"How can a young man keep his way pure? By living by Your Word. I have looked for You with all my heart. Do not let me turn from Your Law. Your Word have I hid in my heart, that I may not sin against You." Psalm 119:9-11

We've all been through heart-break situations and as life goes on it can feel like there are layers of scars and bruises on the inside of us, but we have a choice....We can either let these war wounds make us, or break us. They can make us bitter or better.

I believe God used these difficult situations to make David into the man he was. David kept his heart clean because he knew when he did that he had favour with God.

"In everything he did he had great success, because the Lord was with him." 1 Samuel 18:14

Even when David sinned, his first response was...*"Cleanse my heart!"*

"Create in me a clean heart, O God. Renew a loyal spirit within me." Psalm 51:10 NLT

Perhaps, like David, you feel you've been wronged by other people, or dealt a bad hand in life. Can I encourage you to examine your heart and if needs be respond like David, *"Create in me a clean heart."*

It didn't take long to clean up my computer and it soon started running at full speed again. Let a deep clean take place in your heart. Release forgiveness, eradicate bitterness, isolate insecurities, banish worry. You're precious. Your heart, the real you, the inner you, is where life springs from. So keep it fresh, pure, healed and forgiven.

Prayer: *Heavenly Father, create in me a clean heart, and renew a right spirit within me. I give You my hurts, my bruises, my broken heart and ask You to cleanse me of all unrighteousness. I forgive those who have hurt me and trust that You will vindicate me and put things right.*

THE GRACIOUS HAND OF MY GOD

Jarrod Cooper

"The gracious hand of my God upon me" Nehemiah 2:18

When I think of hands being laid on me, I usually think of getting a smack as a kid, fighting or being chosen to do something I don't want to do!

But this verse makes me think of something else altogether. *"The gracious hand of my God was upon me"* conjures up a vision of the might of heaven, empowering, sustaining and helping me.

"My hand will sustain him; surely my arm will strengthen him." Psalm 89:21.

Oh I want the hand of God to rest on me, how about you?

I think of Hands of Protection. The Bible says *"He hems me in behind and before" Psalm 139:5.*

I remember being chased by men with guns in Zimbabwe, hiding behind the tail of a pick-up truck, praying, terrified but cared for by God. I remember a friend being guarded by visible angels as her car was pulled over by thugs. I remember the whispers of God's Spirit getting me to change plans for a trip, only to hear of a massive explosion at the time I had been due to be there. His hands protect us.

I think of Hands of Power; *"His mighty hand"* took the Israelites through the Red Sea (Psalm 136:12). His hands clear the way, smash through walls, lower mountains, obliterate enemies!

I have seen God's hand overwhelm lives for whom no human intervention was now possible. The sickness was too far gone, the injury beyond repair. But His hands did it! He has literally freed prisoners from captivity, lifted the dying from their death beds and provided for the rejected and the lost.

The same hands that have formed burning suns a billion times bigger than the earth, also formed little Adam's body by his fingertips, setting in place the lenses in Adam's eyes and the miniscule bones of his ears. God's hands are both powerful, and intricately accurate, for me and you.

Finally, I also think of Hands of Approval; *"I have chosen you"* God says, standing like a Father, hands proudly on the shoulders of His growing son. Perhaps nothing is as healing as approval, and you need to know today, God approves, loves, understands, and is deeply committed to you.

Just think of it, the hands of God, *"where His power hides"* as Habakkuk 3:4 puts it, have been placed on your life, imparting God's strength, God's spiritual DNA, God's wisdom and approval.

Surely we must say, *"If God be for me, who can be against me"* Romans 8:31.

Prayer: *Thank You God that Your hand is upon me. The hands of Your protection surround me, the hands of Your power support me, and the hands of Your approval place the seal of Your family on my life today. I confess that You are for me, so who can be against me today!*

FACTS VERSES TRUTH
Marion Cooper

*"The weapons we fight with are not the weapons of the world, on
the contrary, they have power to demolish strongholds.
We demolish arguments and every pretension that sets itself up
against the knowledge of God. And we take every thought captive."*
2 Corinthians 10:5

Just a few years ago I had the opportunity to practice these few
words and to understand them in a new way.

I had found an abnormality in my breast and after ignoring it for
some months, decided perhaps I should see my GP. She, in turn,
thought she may have found a small lump and referred me to the
breast clinic.
It was during the week of waiting and honestly unconcerned, that
God dropped a Bible verse very clearly into my heart.

"Though you will search for your enemies you will not find them."
Isaiah 41.12

I thanked God and continued unconcerned until a week later I
visited the clinic.

Over a period of a couple of hours, I was passed from doctors, to
mammogram and then on to have a scan.

The scan seemed to take a long time, but still I remained at peace
until eventually the practitioner turned 2 screens so I could see
them and said the mammogram and now the scan had picked up
suspicious tissue, she was concerned and wanted to bring in a

colleague. She left the room and it was as I lay alone on the examination couch, that I felt a bubble of fear begin to rise from the pit of my stomach and the thought began to form, *"What if...?"*

I took that embryonic thought and with all the spiritual strength I could muster, I squeezed the very life out of it, I would allow it to go no further.

Inside my head and occasionally whispering out loud, I began to declare the promise God had tucked into my heart just a few days earlier, in preparation for this moment.

"Lord you have said, though I search for my enemies, I will not find them." Over and over I repeated His promise. A couple of biopsies were immediately taken and I went home to wait 3 weeks for the results.

Here are the facts:- Several doctors and tests had found suspicious tissue and other staff were brought in to consult. Fact:- Christians get cancer and even die of cancer.

We cannot ignore the facts, but in the opposite corner is the Truth:- God had said, *"though you search for your enemies you will not find them."*

The facts versus the truth, it was a battle I had to win, perhaps for my health but certainly for my spiritual well being. How disappointed I would feel if I spent these weeks in fear and dread instead of believing the clear word God had planted in my heart.

For the next 3 weeks, I refused to let any negative thought come in to my mind, when it tried, I strangled the life from it and declared God's truth for me, *"Lord You have said..."*
Not once did I allow myself to think I had cancer, standing on that

word day and night, I have no idea how many times I spoke out the truth.

Three weeks later I was declared cancer free!

I was so proud of myself and God allowed me that pride for about 3 days then He challenged me, *"That Marion, is how to take every thought captive and to get the victory over other conflict areas in your life, over fear, worry, stress and anxiety."*

God plants the truth of His word into our hearts and John 8.32 says, *'You shall know the truth and the truth will set you free.'*

Prayer: *Thank You for Your word Father God. It is life and health to my bones. Your word is truth and the truth sets me free. I choose to take every negative, wrong, fearful thought captive and make it obedient to Christ. Because of Jesus I am victorious! I am on the winning side! Your word is powerful, a two edged sword in my hand. I choose to align myself with Your word. I choose to believe and confess the word of God over my life!*

GRIT & DETERMINATION
Victoria Cooper

"We are hard pressed on every side, but not crushed; perplexed, but not in despair." 2 Corinthians 4:8 NIV

One Christmas I was skiing with my family in the French Alps. I was a fairly new skier and very much happy to stick to easy runs (greens and blues) and enjoy the experience rather than join the adrenaline junkies carving up red and black runs (…I really don't need the stress!)

On the other side of the mountain where we were based was a new area of pistes that we really wanted to ski to, but to get there I was faced with a ski run that was a lot harder and steeper than I could master.

Each day I attempted to ski down this piste, but every time ended up sliding down on my bottom! It scared me and stressed me out! Whatever I tried, this difficult run was defeating me and did so right up to the very last day on the mountain when something remarkable happened…

We had been happily skiing in our resort on the last day of our Christmas holiday when suddenly all three of us tumbled into a heap at the top of a ski lift! I fell, injuring myself quite badly. I was gutted and very, very annoyed!

I was angered by my injury, annoyed at the person who caused my injury, (mainly myself, but a little person was involved who will remain nameless). I was irritated at the fact it was our last day, I was now in considerable pain, and I hadn't yet conquered the difficult piste to ski over to the other side of the mountain which had been our challenge for that day.

After spending a few moments sulking and feeling sorry for myself something in me changed. I found that my annoyance became my determination. I strapped up my injury, put my skis back on and headed back up the mountain.

I didn't care if I fell, if I got hurt (again), or if it took me all day. I was going to conquer this nemesis which my 8 year old breezed down with such ease.

I can be super stubborn when I want to be and today I was not going to give up. I ignored my fear and my pain and I went for it.

I gradually snaked down the piste with grit and determination, with my family at the bottom cheering me on. I finally started to get a rhythm as I skied back and forth….. and then I started to sing.

"1,2,3,(turn)1,2,3 (turn) "Oh come let us a-(turn) dore Him" (turn) "Oh come let us a- (turn) dore Him" (turn)."

My skiing started to feel like a dance, the fear and the stress left me and the rhythm and the song took over me. I MADE IT! After that I tackled a red run and even part of a black run!

I'm sharing this story because I've learnt in life that if you're going to step into destiny, you're going to have to conquer some fears, get hurt, trip up and sometimes fall flat on your face a few times.

You've got to get pig sick with where you're at, strap up your wounds, climb the mountain and face your fears head on.

I have a little mantra that I wear on a bracelet and have plastered on my office wall. You may have heard it before....It says,

"Life isn't about waiting for the storm to pass, it's learning to dance in the rain."

You're never going to escape injury or the fear of falling. People will still hurt you and let you down, difficult situations will come and go.....but it's pointless worrying or even sulking about it.

When Paul was in prison he was at an all time low.....but what did he do? He chose to sing through his pain and his fears, and look what happened....

"Around midnight Paul and Silas were praying and singing hymns to God, and the other prisoners were listening. Suddenly, there was a massive earthquake, and the prison was shaken to its foundations. All the doors immediately flew open, and the chains of every prisoner fell off!" Acts 16:25-26 NLT

I'm not belittling what you've been through or what you're currently going through, but at some point it's time to strap up your hurts, pain, injures and start moving again, start climbing, take a step of faith, get your rhythm back, start singing, praising and thanking God as you ride the great adventure God had destined for you.

Action Point: *Think through areas in your life you have shied away from because you got hurt or scared. Pray through what God wants you to do and start to make some steps towards fulfilling your destiny.*

ABOUT THE AUTHORS

Jarrod Cooper is the Senior Leader of Revive Church, a multi-site church based in East Yorkshire. Inspirational in style, he uses speech, song, worship and prophetic ministry, in a "sometimes challenging" and "often humorous" way to encourage the Church to reach higher in God. This work has taken him throughout the UK, Europe, Africa and America since 1990, speaking at churches, conferences, on television and radio and through writing and producing training and coaching materials.

Victoria Cooper has a passion for Presence-filled creativity that touches the hearts of everyone! With experience in dance, and having overseen productions, concerts and shows that have been touched by God's presence and that have led many to Christ, Vicky's heart to coach creatives to fullness in God, will inspire you through her work in Revive Academy which she co-leads with her husband.

Together, their main passion is that *"the glory of the Lord would cover the earth, as the waters cover the sea,"* and they seek to lift believers to a life in the supernatural, that will display God's presence and power in every day life.

Marion Cooper, along with her husband David have been in ministry since the 1970's, firstly in church eldership in Newport, South Wales, followed by 10 years as missionaries leading a church in Gibraltar. On return to the UK in 1988 they became senior leaders of Revive Church (called "New Life Church" at the time) and led the church until 2005. Now officially retired they continue to speak, travel, support leaders and write, but also have lots of fun with their grandson, Zachary. They have two grown sons, Jason and Jarrod.

ALSO BY JARROD COOPER

Books:
500: Are we at the dawn of a new era of glory?
Believe & Confess (with Victoria Cooper)
When Spirit & Word Collide
Glory in the Church

Online Courses:
When Spirit & Word Collide
STRONGER
Moving in Healing, Miracles & Prophecy
Living Free from Stress, Anxiety & Depression

Music:
Sanctuary

Download a FREE worship album by Jarrod from:
JarrodCooper.net

To keep up to date with news from Jarrod & Victoria or to follow their blogs, download free podcasts or purchase their products visit their website www.jarrodcooper.net

Printed in Great Britain
by Amazon

31870836R00119